PIANO • VOCAL • GUITAR

BIG BOOK of STANDARDS

This publication is not for sale in the E.C. and/or Australia or New Zealand.

ISBN 0-7935-3238-8

BIG BOOK of STANDARDS

CONTENTS

CONTENTS

ALL ALONE

Words and Music by
IRVING BERLIN

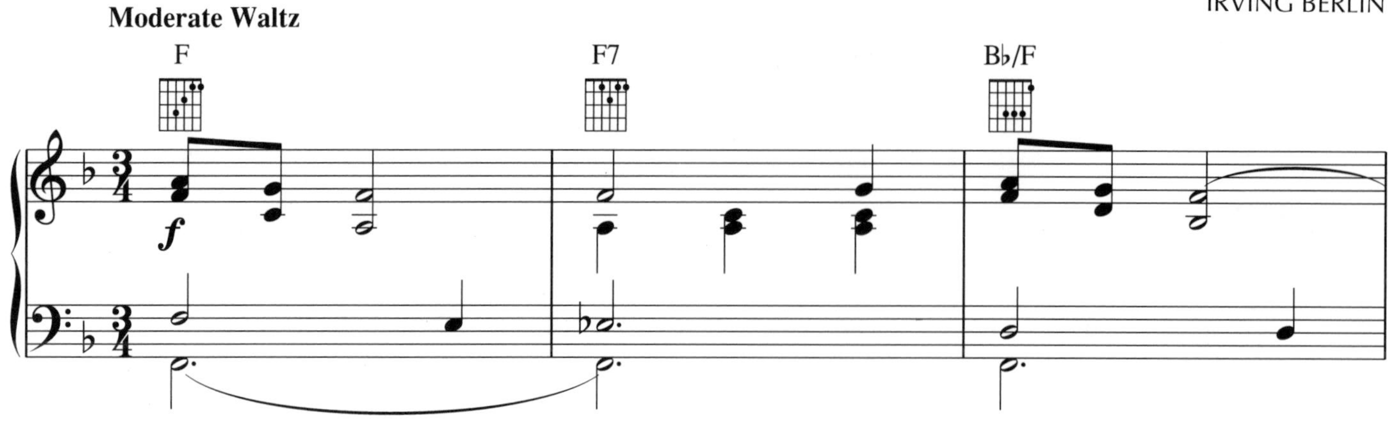

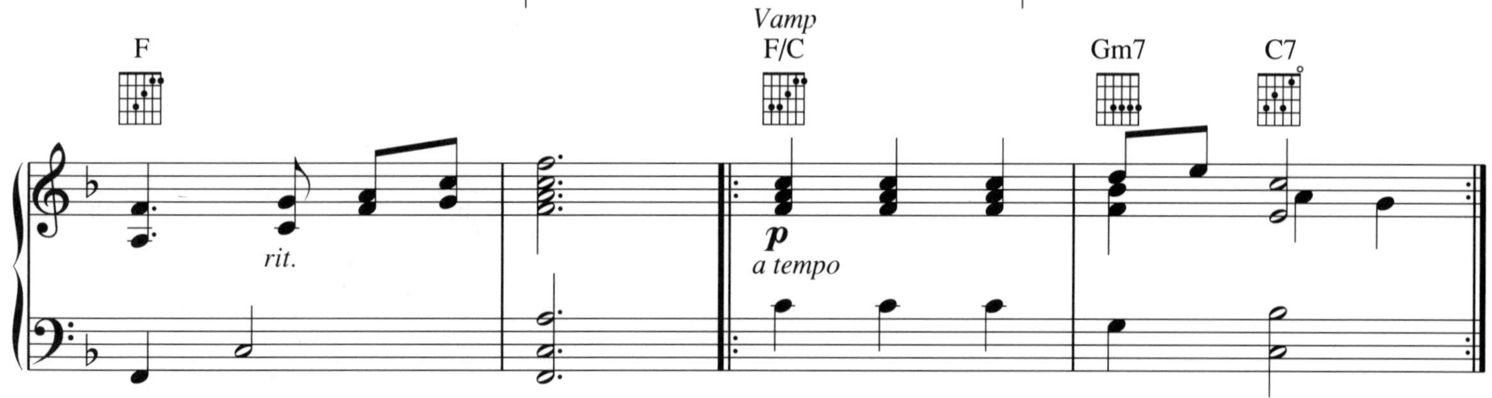

Gm/D
C7
C+
F
F/C
you seem to haunt me night and day.
you seemed to van - ish like a dream.
Dm
F7
Am/E
F♯m7♭5
I nev - er re - al - ized till you had gone
I long to hold you in my arms a - gain.
F7♭5
E7
Am
F♯dim7
Gm7
C7
how much I cared a - bout you. I can't live with - out you.
My life is ver - y lone - ly, for I want you on - ly.
rall.
F
F/C
C7
All a - lone, I'm so all a - lone. There is
a tempo

F
C7♯5
F
F/C
no one else but you.
C7
A7
Dm
All a - lone by the tel - e - phone wait - ing
A/E
E7
Am
for a ring, a ting - a -
C7
F7
B♭
ling. I'm all a - lone ev - 'ry eve - ning,

B♭7
G7
C7
C7♭9
all a - lone feel - ing blue,
rall.
C7
C7♯5
F
F7
B♭/F
won - d'ring where you are, and how you are
a tempo
Gm7♭5
F/C
C7
and if you are, all a - lone
rall.
1
F
A♭dim7
Gm7
C7♯5
2
F
too.
too.
a tempo

APRIL IN PARIS

Words by E.Y. HARBURG
Music by VERNON DUKE

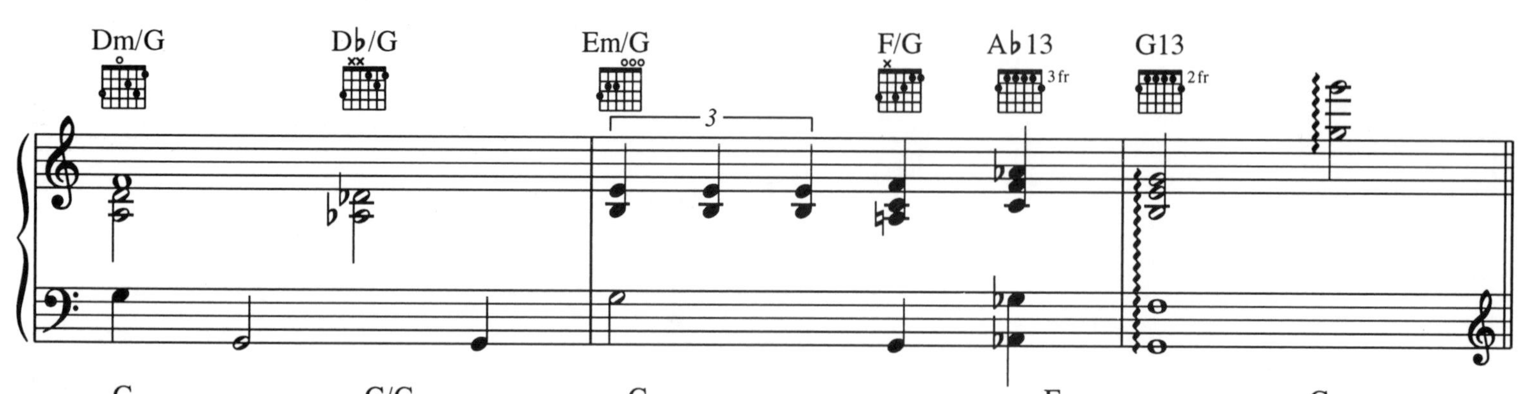

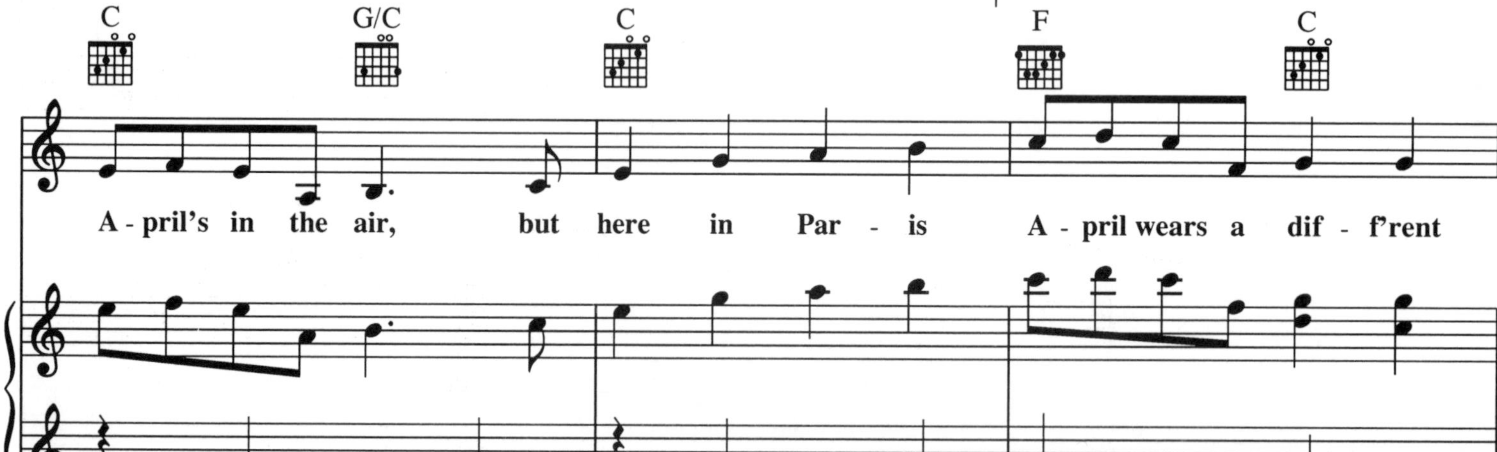

E♭6
Dm7
G13
G7♯5
C
G/C
street. The tang of wine is in the air, I'm
C
F
Em7
Bm7♭5
drunk with all the hap - pi - ness that Spring can give.
E7/B
A13
D9
Nev - er dreamed it could be so ex - cit - ing to
Dm7/G
G7
live.

Fm6/G
B6/G
C6/G
C6
Dm7♭5
D♯m/G
G13
A - pril in Par - is,
Chest - nuts in blos - som,
Cmaj9
B
C
Hol - i - day ta - bles un - der the trees.
Gm7
C9
F6
Fdim7
Fmaj7
A - pril in Par - is,
Em7
G♯dim7
Am7
This is a feel - ing

F#m7♭5
B7#5
B7
E7#5
E7
no - one can ev - er re - prise.
Em7♭5
A7
Fmaj7
Fdim7
C/E
E♭dim7
I nev - er knew the charm of Spring,
Ddim7
Fm6
C/E
E+
Bm7♭5
E7
Nev - er met it face to face. I nev - er knew my
Am
F#m7♭5
B7
B7#5
Emaj7
Dm7
G7
heart could sing, Nev - er missed a warm em - brace, till

Fm6/G
B6/G
C6/G
C6
Em7♭5
E+
A7♯5
A - pril in Par - is,
whom can I run to,
D13
Ddim7
D9
G7
What have you done to my
1
C6
G13
heart?
2
A♭maj7
D♭maj7
C6
heart?

AUTUMN IN NEW YORK

Words and Music by
VERNON DUKE

Bbm7
Eb9
Ab
4fr
pose of my rose col - ored chat - tels and pre -
Bb7
Eb7#5(b9)
5fr
Cm7b5
C7sus
C7
pare for my share of ad - ven - tures and bat - tles.
F
Gm7b5
5fr
F6/9
Gm7b5
5fr
Here on my twen - ty - sev - enth floor, look - ing down on the cit - y I
Db7
4fr
C7#5
G+/F
Gb+/C
F+
C7#5
hate and a - dore!

Liltingly and Freely
Gm7
Am7
B♭6
C7
C7♯5
Au - tumn in New York, why does it seem so in - vit - ing?
Au - tumn in New York, the gleam - ing roof - tops at sun - down.
mf
F
Dm7
Am7
D7♭9(♯11)
D9♯11
Gm7
Am7
Au - tumn in New York,
Au - tumn in New York,
B♭6
C7
C7♯5
Am7♭5
D7
it spells the thrill of first night - ing.
it lifts you up when you're run - down.
Gm7
B♭m7
E♭7
A♭maj7
Glit - ter - ing crowds and shim - mer - ing clouds in can - yons of steel,
Jad - ed rou - és and gay di - vorc - ees who lunch at the Ritz,

Dm7♭5
Cm/G
Cm/D
3fr
G7♯5
they're making me feel I'm
will tell you that "it's di-
C
C7
C7♯5
Gm7
Am7
home. It's autumn in New York
vine!" This autumn in New York
B♭6
F
Dm7
D9♯11
4fr
D♭9
that brings the promise of new love;
transforms the slums into Mayfair;
Cm7
E♭m7
F7
Autumn in New York is often mingled with
Autumn in New York, you'll need no castles in

Bbm7
Gb/Bb
Bbm6
Fm
C7#5
C7
pain.
Spain.
Dream-ers with emp - ty
Lov - ers that bless the
Fm
Ab7
Ab7#5
Db
Ab7
Ab7#5
Db
Db9
hands may sigh for ex - o - tic lands; It's
dark on bench - es in Cen - tral Park greet
Gm7
Am7
Bbm6
C7susb9
C7b9
Fm
Au - tumn in New York, it's good to live it a - gain.
Au - tumn in New York; it's good to live it a -
C7
Fm
Eb9
Fm6
gain.
p

BEYOND THE BLUE HORIZON

(From The Paramount Picture "MONTE CARLO")

Words by LEO ROBIN
Music by RICHARD A. WHITING
and W. FRANKE HARLING

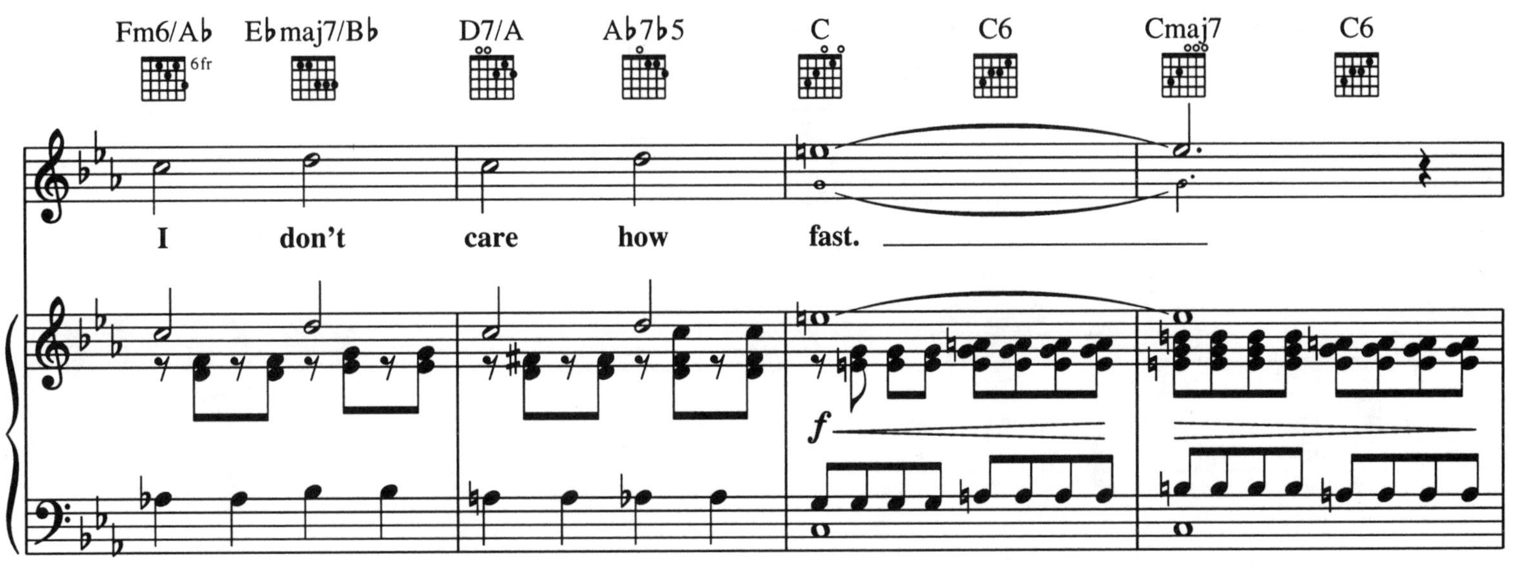
Fm6/A♭
6fr
E♭maj7/B♭
D7/A
A♭7♭5
C
C6
Cmaj7
C6
I don't care how fast.
f

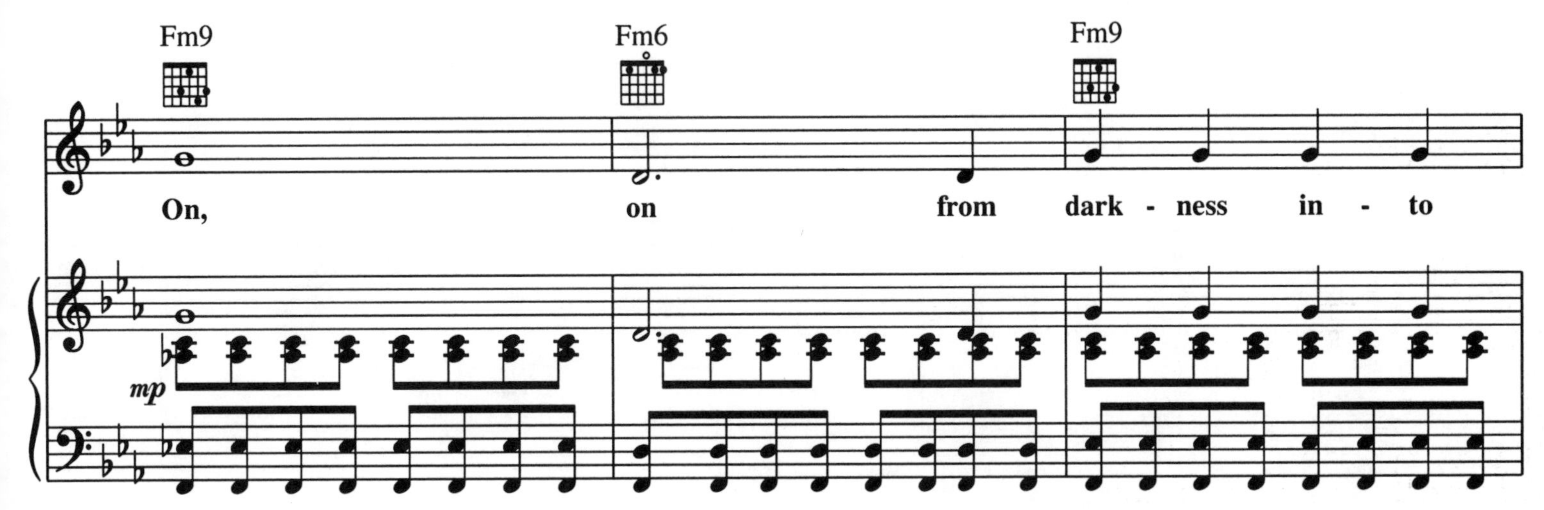
Fm9
Fm6
Fm9
On, on from dark - ness in - to
mp

Fm6
B♭9
E♭6
dawn, from rain in - to the rain - bow,

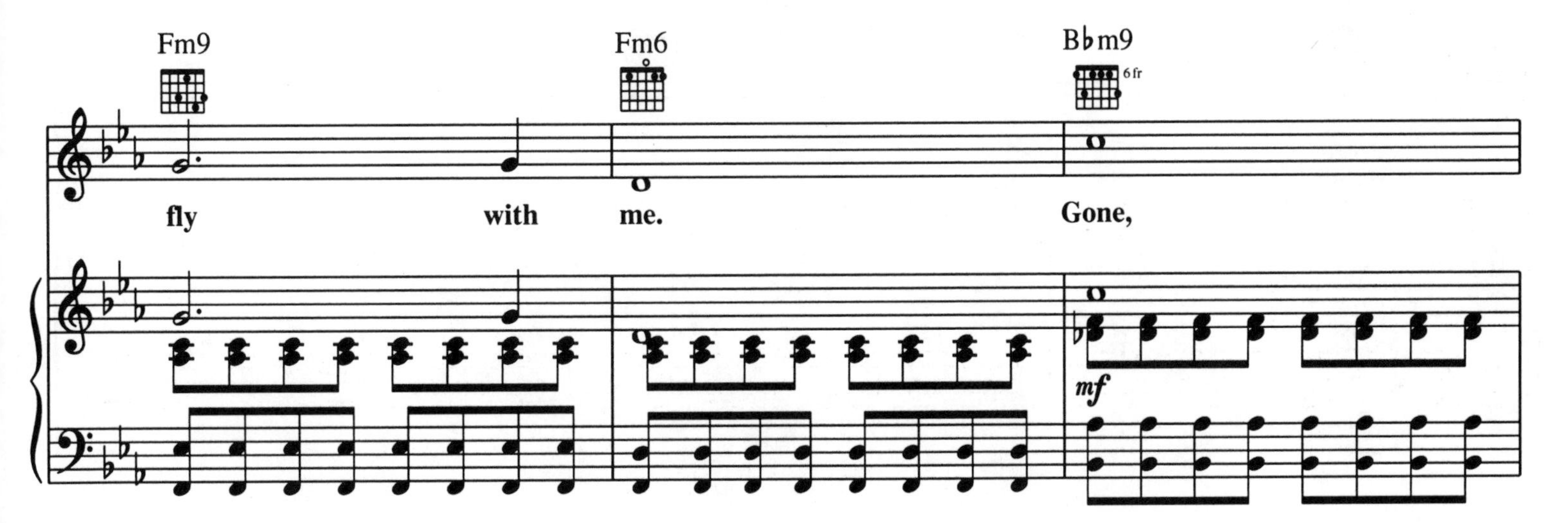
Fm9
Fm6
B♭m9
6fr
fly with me. Gone,
mf

E♭9
B♭m9
E♭9
gone all my grief and woe. What
D9
E♭9
D9
E♭9
mat - ter where I go if I am free?
Moderately (In 2)
no chord
Be -
mp rall.
Moderately fast
A♭
A♭dim7
A♭
D♭m
E♭7
yond the blue ho - ri - zon

Ab
Abdim7
Ab
F9
F9#5
F9
waits a beau - ti - ful day.
Good -
R.H.
Bbm7
Dbm
Ab/C
Bdim7
bye to things that bore me.
Bb7
Eb7
Eb7#5
Joy is wait - ing for me. I
Ab
Abdim7
Ab
Dbm
Eb7
see a new ho - ri - zon.

Ab
Cdim7
F7
Cm7/G
My life has on - ly be - gun.
Abm6
F7/A
Bbm
Bbm7b5
Bbm7
Be - yond the blue ho -
Dbm
Ab/Eb
Edim7
Fm
Bbm7
Eb7
ri - zon lies a ris - ing
mf

1
Ab
Bbm9
Eb9#5
2
Ab
Db/Eb
Ab
sun. Be - sun.
mp

BEYOND THE SEA

F Dm B♭ C F Dm B♭ C
where Be-yond The Sea {He's / She's} there watch-ing for
F A7 Dm C7 F Dm
me, If I could fly like birds on
B♭ D7 Gm C7 Dm B♭ Gm7 C7
high, then straight to {his / her} arms I'd go sail -
F E7 A F♯m7 D E7 A F♯m7
ing. It's far be-yond a star, it's
Bm E7 A G7
near be-yond the moon, I

C Am F G7 C Am7 Dm G7
know beyond a doubt, my heart will lead me there
C C7 Am C7 F Dm Bb C7
soon. We'll meet beyond the
F Dm Bb C7 F A7 Dm C7
shore, we'll kiss just as before, Happy we'll
F Dm Bb D7 Gm C7 Dm Bb
be Beyond The Sea and never again I'll go
G7 C7 F Gm7 C7 G7 C7 F
sail - ing. Some - sail - ing.

BLAME IT ON MY YOUTH

Words by EDWARD HEYMAN
Music by OSCAR LEVANT

Eb
Gm
Bb7
Eb
Fm7
Bb7
throw a - way.
If I ex - pect - ed love
Eb
B7
Bb7
Edim7
Fm7
Bb7
when first we kissed, Blame it on my youth;
Fm7
C#dim7
Fm7
Bb7
Eb
Fm7
Bb7
If on - ly just for you I did ex - ist, Blame it on my youth.
Eb
Db
Eb7
Ab
Bb7
Eb
I be - lieved in ev - 'ry - thing

Fm7 Gm A♭ G7♯5 G7 C7♭9 C7 Fm7 B♭7
Like a child of three, You meant more than
G7♯5 G7 C7♭9 C7 F9 B7♯5 B♭7
an - y - thing, All the world to me!
E♭ Fm7 B♭7 E♭ B7 B♭7 Edim
If you were on my mind all night and day, Blame it on my youth;
Fm7 B♭7 Fm7 C♯dim Fm7 B♭7
If I for - got to eat and sleep and

E♭ Fm7 B♭7 E♭ D♭ E♭7 A♭ B♭7
pray, Blame it on my youth. If I cried a
E♭ Edim Fm7 G7♯5 G7 C7♭9 C7
lit - tle bit When first I learned the truth,
Fm7 C♯dim7 Fm7 F9 E♭ B♭7 E♭ Edim
Don't blame it on my heart, Blame it on my youth.
Fm7 B♭7 E♭ Fm7♭5 E♭

THE BLUE ROOM
(From "THE GIRL FRIEND")

Words by LORENZ HART
Music by RICHARD RODGERS

B♭
Fmaj7
B♭
F
broth - er's room, On the wall are two prints.
8va
B♭
F
D7
Gm
3fr
D7
Here's the kid - dies' room, Here's the
Gm
3fr
D7
Gm7
3fr
C7
bid - dy's room, Here's a pan - try lined with
F6
C7
Fmaj7
B♭
Fmaj7
shelves, dear, Here I've planned for us, Some - thing

B♭
Fmaj7
B♭
B♭maj7/A
6fr
Gm7
3fr
C7
grand for us, Where we two can be our - selves, dear,
rall.
Slowly, with expression
F
C7
F
We'll have a blue room, a new room, For
C7
F
Fmaj7
F7
B♭
Gm7
3fr
two room, Where ev - 'ry day's a hol - i - day Be -
F
G7
C7
F
cause you're mar - ried to me. Not like a

C7
F
C7
ball - room A small room, A hall room, Where
F
Fmaj7
F7
B♭
Gm7
3 fr
F
Gm7
3 fr
C7
I
you
can smoke
my
your
pipe a - way, With
your
my
wee head up - on
my
your
L.H.
F
C7
knee. We will thrive on, keep a - live on
F
C7
Just noth - ing but kiss - es, With Mis - ter and

Gm7
3fr
C7
Dm7
G7
C7
Mis - sus On lit - tle blue chairs.
F
C7
F
You sew your
I'll wear my
trous - seau, And Rob - in - son
C7
F
Fmaj7
F7
B♭
Gm7
3fr
Cru - soe Is not so far from world - ly cares As our
F
Gm7
3fr
C7
1
F
Gm7
3fr
C7
2
F
blue room far a - way up - stairs!
stairs!
poco rall.
rit.

BLUE SKIES

Words and Music by
IRVING BERLIN

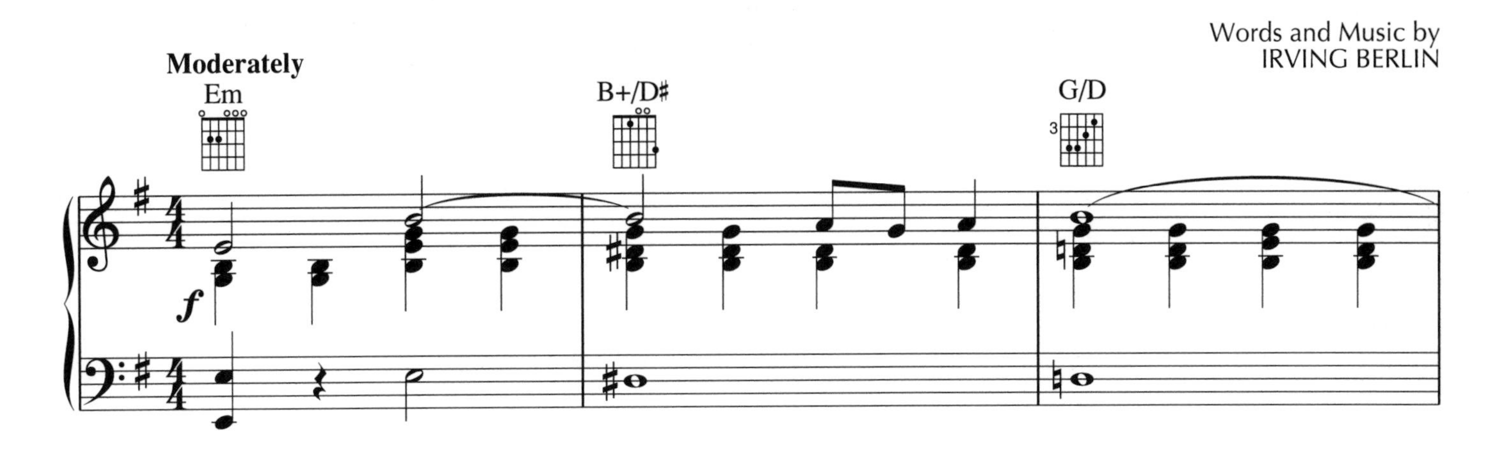

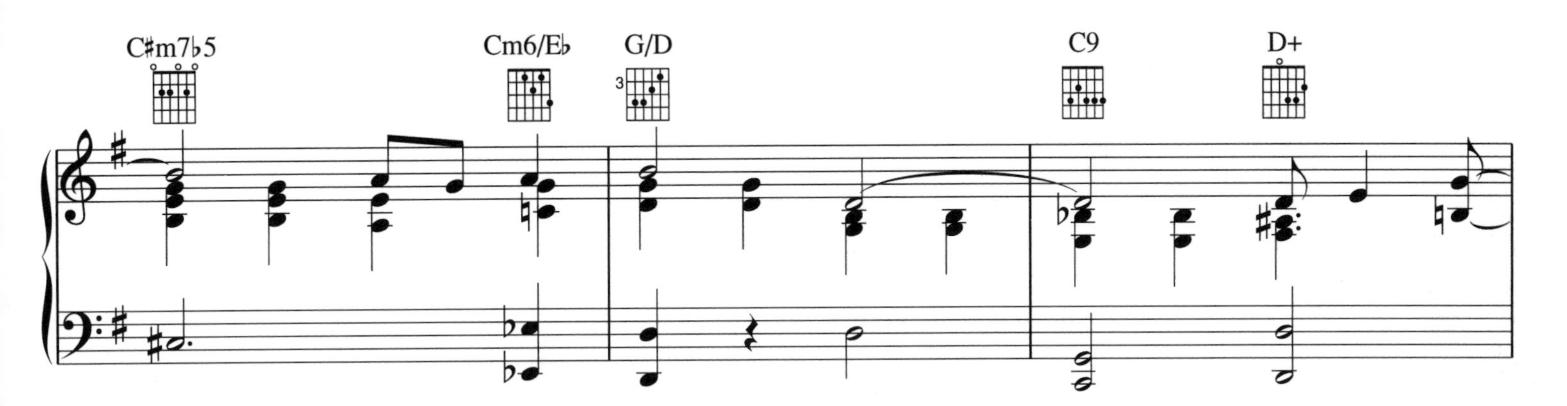

G
G7
be.
west.
Ev - 'ry day was a
I should fret if the
C6/G
G6
Gm6
A7
cloud - y day for me.
worst looks like the best.
Bm
F#+
F#7
D7
C#7/D
Then good luck came a - knock - ing at my door.
I should mind if they say it can't be true.
D7
G
G7
C6/G
C7
Skies were gray but they're not gray an - y
I should smile that's ex - act - ly what I

G
B+
Em
more.
do.
Blue skies
B+/D♯
B7/D♯
G/D
C♯m7♭5
Cm6/E♭
smil - ing at me.
Noth - ing but
G/D
C9
D+
G
blue skies do I see.
Em
B+/D♯
B7/D♯
Blue - birds sing - ing a

G/D
C♯m7♭5
Cm6/E♭
G/D
song; nothing but blue - birds
C9
D+
G
all day long.
Cm/G
G
Cm/G
G
Nev - er saw the sun shin - ing so bright. Nev - er saw things
Cm/G
G
Cm/G
G
go - ing so right. No - tic - ing the days hur - ry - ing by;

Cm/G
G
D7
G
B+
Em
when you're in love, my how they fly. Blue days,
B+/D♯
B7/D♯
G/D
C♯m7♭5
Cm6/E♭
all of them gone. Noth - ing but
G/D
C9
D+
1
G
blue skies from now on.
2
G
D
G
rit.

BORN FREE

(From The Columbia Pictures' Release "BORN FREE")

Words by DON BLACK
Music by JOHN BARRY

C7
Dm
Dm7
where no walls di - vide you, you're free as a
Dm7-5
B♭m6
C
C7
roar - ing tide, so there's no need to hide.
f
F
B♭
F
B♭
Born free, and life is worth liv - ing, but on - ly worth
f
Am
Gm7
C7sus
F
liv - ing 'cause you're born free.

CALL ME IRRESPONSIBLE

(From The Paramount Picture "PAPA'S DELICATE CONDITION")

Words by SAMMY CAHN
Music by JAMES VAN HEUSEN

Am7
D7♯5
Gm
3fr
Cdim7
C7
Do my fool - ish al - i - bis
Am7♭5
D7♭9
4fr
D+
D7
Dm7/G
G7
bore you? Well, I'm
Gm7/C
not too clev - er. I just a -
R.H.
Gm7
C7
F
F6
F♯dim7
dore you. Call me un - pre - dict - a - ble,

Gm
Gm6
G♯dim7
Fmaj7/A
F
3 fr
tell me I'm im - prac - ti - cal, rain - bows
A7
D7
I'm in - clined to pur - sue.
Gm
Cdim7
C7
3 fr
Call me ir - re - spon - si - ble,

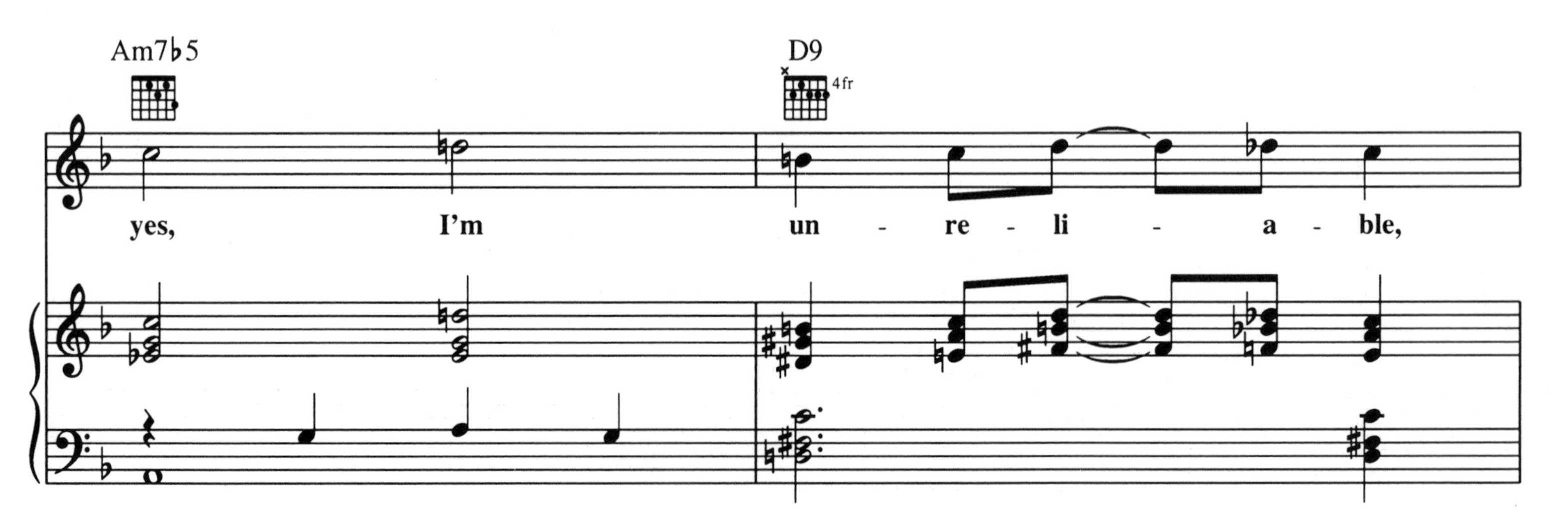
Am7♭5
D9
4 fr
yes, I'm un - re - li - a - ble,

Gm7
Cdim7
C7
but it's un - de - ni - a - bly
A7
D7♭9
4 fr
D7
Gm7
true,
I'm ir - re - spon - si - bly
3
C7♭9
1
F
Gm7/C
Fmaj7
Gm7/C
mad for you!
2
F
Fmaj7
you!
p

CHEEK TO CHEEK
(From The RKO Radio Motion Picture "TOP HAT")

Words and Music by
IRVING BERLIN

A7 Bm/D D7 G7 Dm7 G7/D F/G G9
And I seem to find the hap - pi - ness I
E7/B B♭7♭5 A7 Dm7
seek when we're out to - geth - er danc -
G7 F/G G7 C Cmaj7/E Dm7 G7♯5 F/C C C/G
- ing cheek to cheek. Heav - en,
Dm7 C/G G7 F/C C C/G Dm7 C/G G7
I'm in Heav - en. And the

C
G7/D
D♯dim7
C/E
B♭9♯11
cares that hung a - round me thru the week
A7
Bm/D
D7
G7
Dm7
G7/D
F/G
G9
seem to van - ish like a gamb - ler's luck - y
E7/B
B♭7♭5
A7
Dm7
streak when we're out to - geth - er danc -
G7
F/G
G7
C
Dm7/G
C6
- ing cheek to cheek. Oh, I

G7/D
G7
C6
C/G
G7/D
G7
love to climb a moun - tain, and to reach the high - est peak.
C
C/G
G7/D
G7
C6
C/E
But it does - n't thrill me half as much as
Dm7
G7
C6
C/G
G7/D
G7
danc - ing cheek to cheek. Oh I love to go out fish -
C
C/G
G7/D
G7
C
- ing in a riv - er or a creek. But I

G7/D
G7
C6
C/E
Dm7
G7
C6
don't en - joy it half as much as danc - ing cheek to cheek.
Cm
Cm7
A♭9
3
Dance with me. I want my arm a - bout you.
A♭9/G♭
Fdim7
G7♭9
G♯dim7
Am
C/G
D9/F♯
The charm a - bout you will car - ry me thru
rit.
G7
F/C
C
C/G
Dm7
C/G
G7
F/C
C
C/G
to Heav - en. I'm in Heav - en.

Dm7
C/G
G7
C
G7/D
D♯dim7
C/E
B♭9♯11
And my heart beats so that I can hard - ly speak.
A7
Bm/D
D7
G7
Dm7
G7/D
F/G
G9
E7/B
B♭7♭5
And I seem to find the hap - pi - ness I seek
A7
Dm7
G7
F/G
G7
when we're out to - geth - er danc - ing cheek to cheek.
1
C
E♭dim7
Dm
G7
2
C
Dm7/G
C6

CHERRY PINK AND APPLE BLOSSOM WHITE

French Words by JACQUES LARUE
English Words by MACK DAVID
Music by LOUIGUY

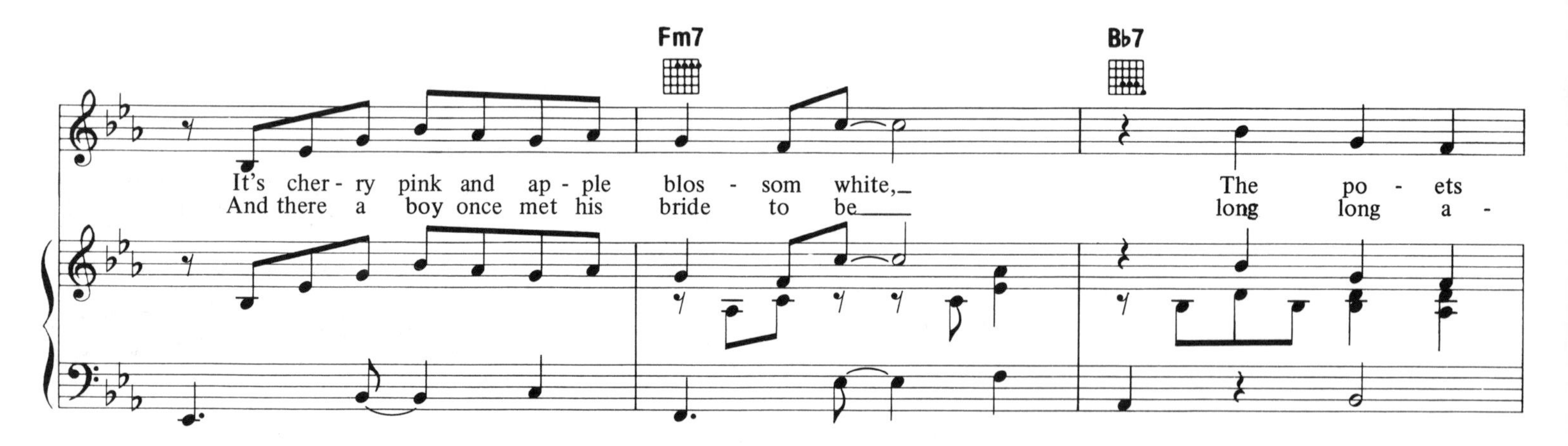

Bb7
Eb
Bb7
Eb
in-to her eyes, It was a sight to en-thrall, The breez-es joined in their sighs, The blos-soms start-ed to fall. And as they

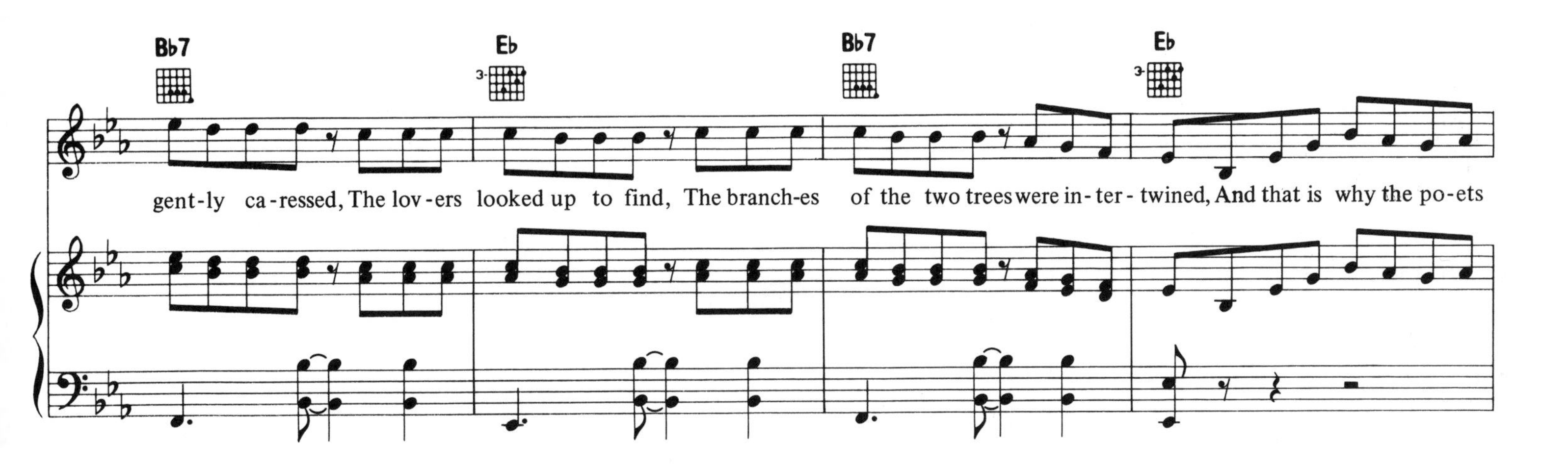
Bb7
Eb
Bb7
Eb
gent-ly ca-ressed, The lov-ers looked up to find, The branch-es of the two trees were in-ter-twined, And that is why the po-ets

Fm7
Bb7
Eb
al - ways write,
If there's a new moon bright a - bove,
It's cher-ry pink and ap - ple

Fm7
Bb7
Eb
blos - som white,
When you're in love.

COCKTAILS FOR TWO

(From The Paramount Picture "MURDER AT THE VANITIES")

Words and Music by ARTHUR JOHNSTON
and SAM COSLOW

E
B7+
E
A9
A7-9
civ - il - ized la - dies and men.
No long - er need we miss
rall.
Dm7
Moderately Fast
G
F♯
G
F♯
G
D7+
G7
a charm - ing scene like this.
rall.
Refrain
Moderately Slow and Expressively
C
B7
C6
Tacet
In some se - clud - ed ren - dez - vous,
that o - ver - looks the av - e -
G7
C♯dim
G7
Tacet
Dm7
G7
Dm7
G7
nue,
with some - one shar - ing a de - light - ful chat of this and that and

Cmaj7
Cm6
G7
Tacet
C6
B7
cock-tails for two.
As we en-joy a cig-a-rette
C6
Tacet
G7
C♯dim
G7
Tacet
to some ex-qui-site chan-son-nette,
two hands are sure to sly-ly
Dm7
G7
Dm7
G7
C9
B7+
C7
Fmaj7
F6
meet be-neath a ser-vi-ette with cock-tails for two.
My head may go reel-ing,
Fm6
C
F♯dim
Dm7
G7
but my heart will be o-be-di-ent,
with in-tox-i-cat-ing kiss-es for the

G9 G7 C6 C♯dim G7 Tacet C6 B7
prin - ci-pal in-gre - di-ent. Most an-y aft - er - noon at five
C6 Tacet G7 C♯dim G7 Tacet
we'll be so glad we're both a - live. Then may - be for - tune will com -

Dm7 G7 Dm7 G7 1. C7 F6 A♭7 C Tacet
plete her plan that all be-gan with cock-tails for two. In some se-clud-ed ren-dez -

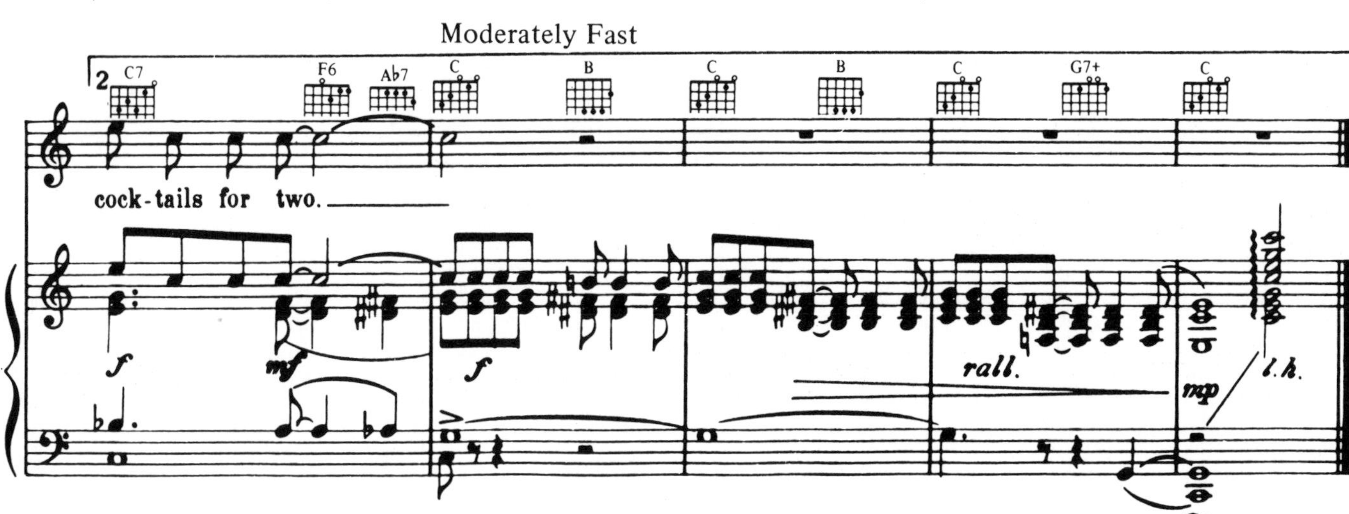
Moderately Fast
2. C7 F6 A♭7 C B C B C G7+ C
cock-tails for two.
rall.
l.h.

CHEROKEE
(INDIAN LOVE SONG)

Words and Music by
RAY NOBLE

Moderately bright swing

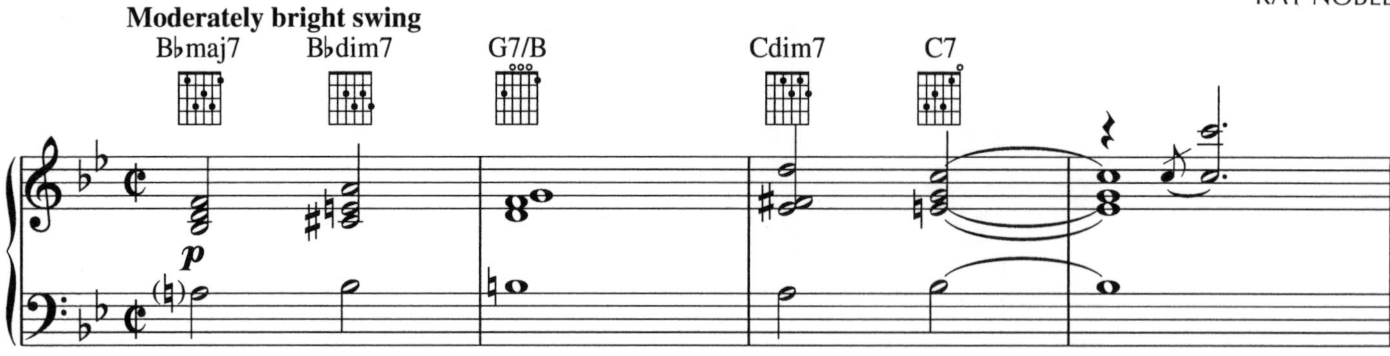

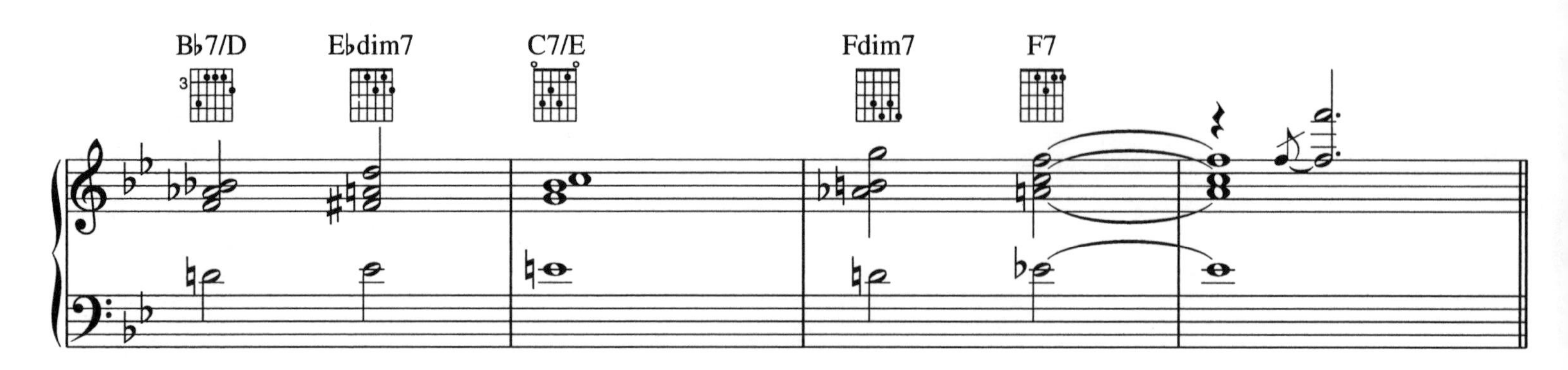

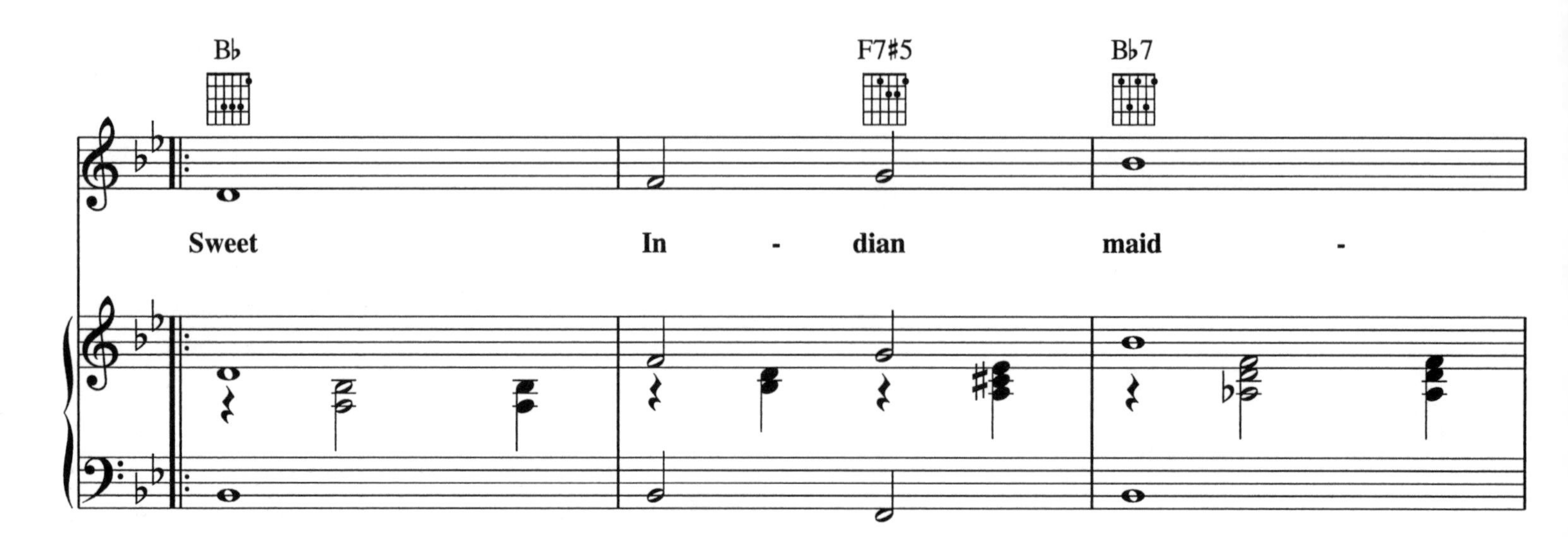

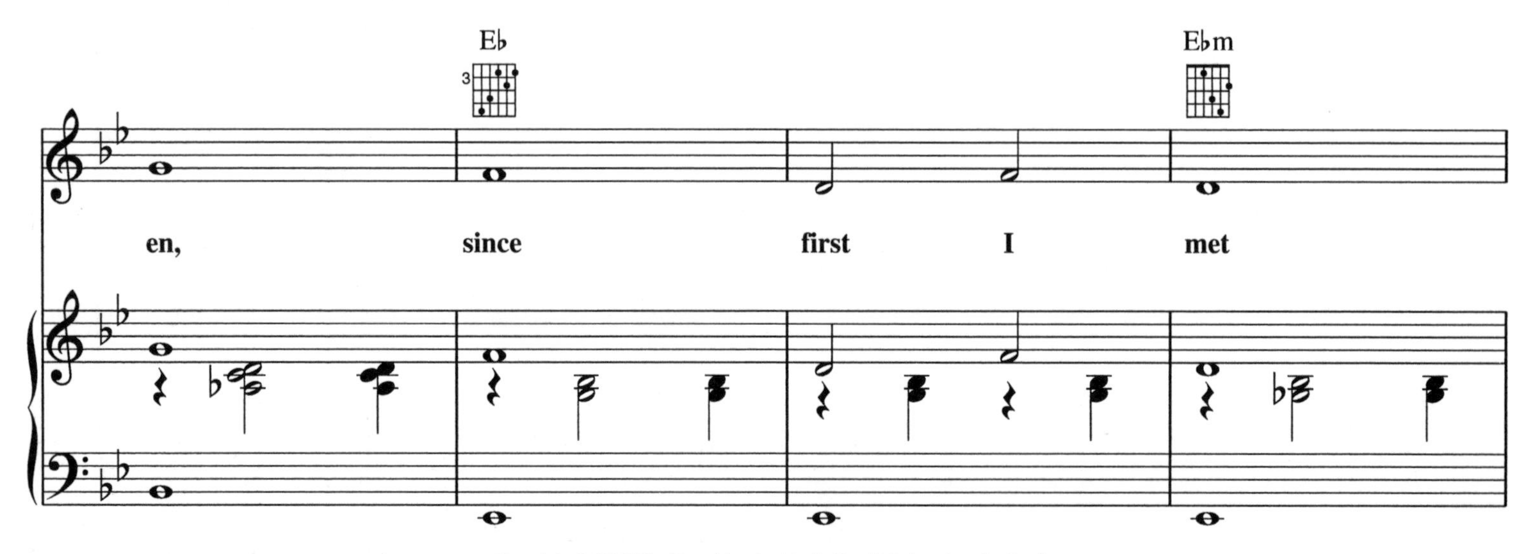

B♭
Dm
C9
you, I can't for - get
Cm7
Fdim
E♭
you, Cher - o - kee sweet -
F7♯5
B♭
F7♯5
B♭7
heart. Child of the prai -
E♭
E♭m
rie, your love keeps call -

B♭
Dm
C9
ing, my heart en - thrall -
Cm7
F7
B♭
ing, Cher - o - kee.
C#m7/F#
F#7
Bmaj7
Dreams of sum - mer - time
B7
Bm7/E
E7
of lov - er - time gone

A
Am7/D
D7
by
throng
my
Gmaj7
G7
Gm7/C
mem - o - ry
so
ten - der - ly
C7
Cm7
F7♯5
and
sigh
my
B♭
F7♯5
B♭7
sweet
in - dian
maid - en

E♭
E♭m
one day I'll hold you,
B♭
Dm
C9
in my arms fold you,
Cm7
F7
1
B♭
Gm
Cher - o - kee.
R.H.
E♭m/G♭
F7
2
B♭
kee.
R.H.
p

DANCE WITH A DOLLY
(WITH A HOLE IN HER STOCKIN')

Words and Music by TERRY SHAND,
JIMMY EATON and MICKEY LEADER

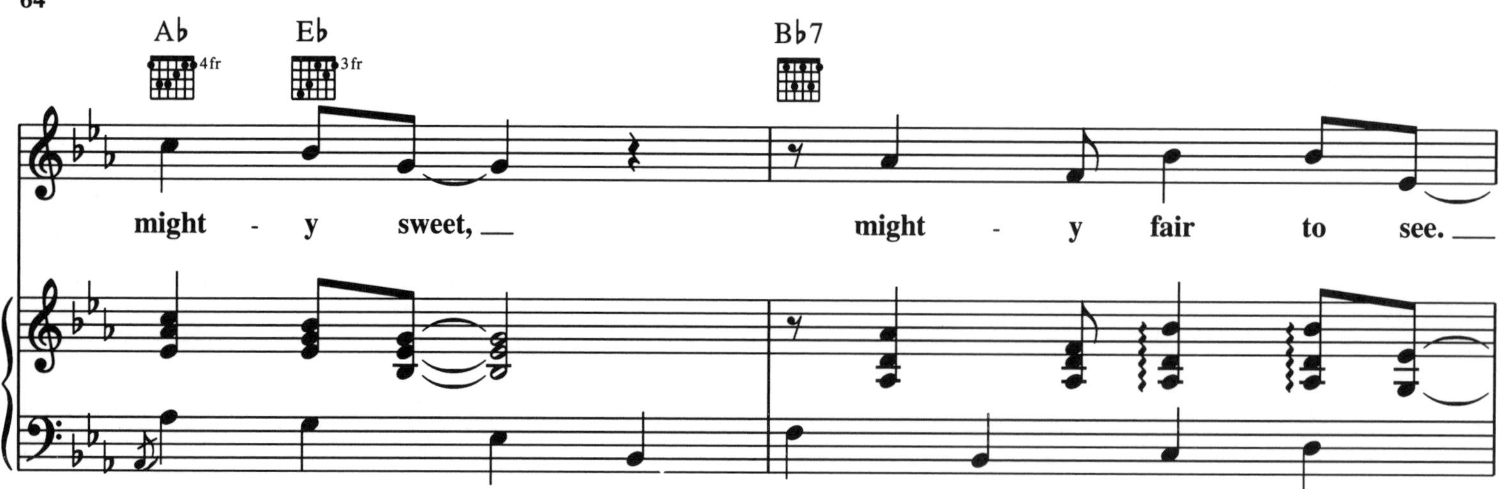
Ab
Eb
4fr
3fr
Bb7
might - y sweet, __ might - y fair to see. __

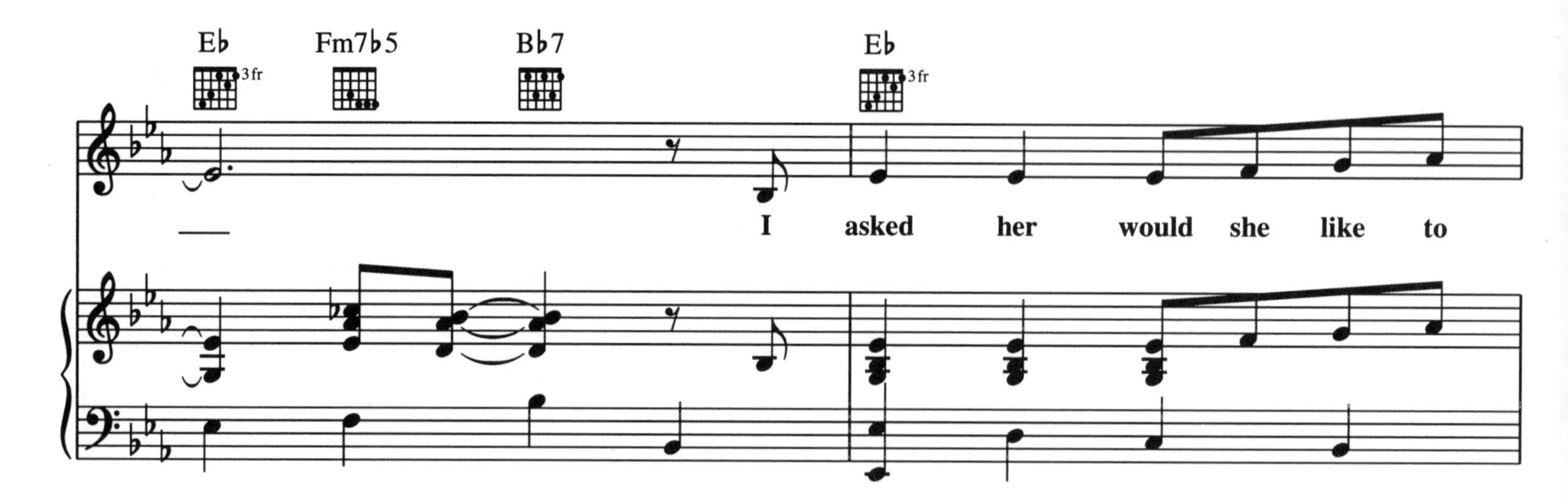
Eb
Fm7b5
Bb7
Eb
3fr
I asked her would she like to

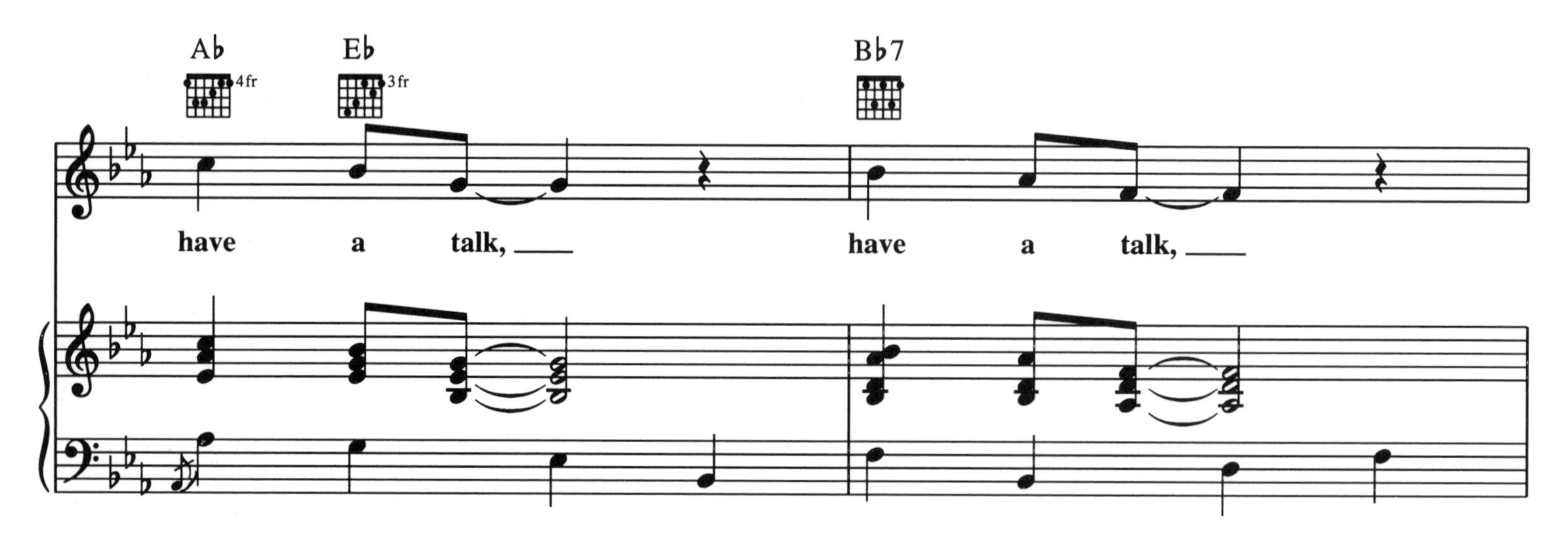
Ab
Eb
4fr
3fr
Bb7
have a talk, __ have a talk, __

Ab/Eb
Eb
3fr
make some talk. All the fel - lows stand - in'

Ab
4fr
Eb
3fr
Bb7
on the walk, wish - in' they were me.
Eb
3fr
Eb7
Ab
4fr
Adim7
Ma - ma, Ma - ma, let me
Ma - ma, Ma - ma, put the
got more kiss - es than a
Eb/Bb
6fr
Eb
3fr
Edim7
Bb7
Eb
3fr
Eb7
dress up to-night, dress up to-night, dress up to-night.
cat out to-night, cat out to-night, cat out to-night.
can - dy store, can - dy store, can - dy store.
Ab
4fr
Adim7
Eb
3fr
I've got a se - cret, gon - na 'fess up to - night. Gon - na
Worked all day. I'm gon - na scat out to - night and I
Sweet - er than I've ev - er had be - fore, still I

F7
Bb7
dance by the light of the moon.
won't be home un - til dawn.
keep on cry - in' for more.
Gon - na

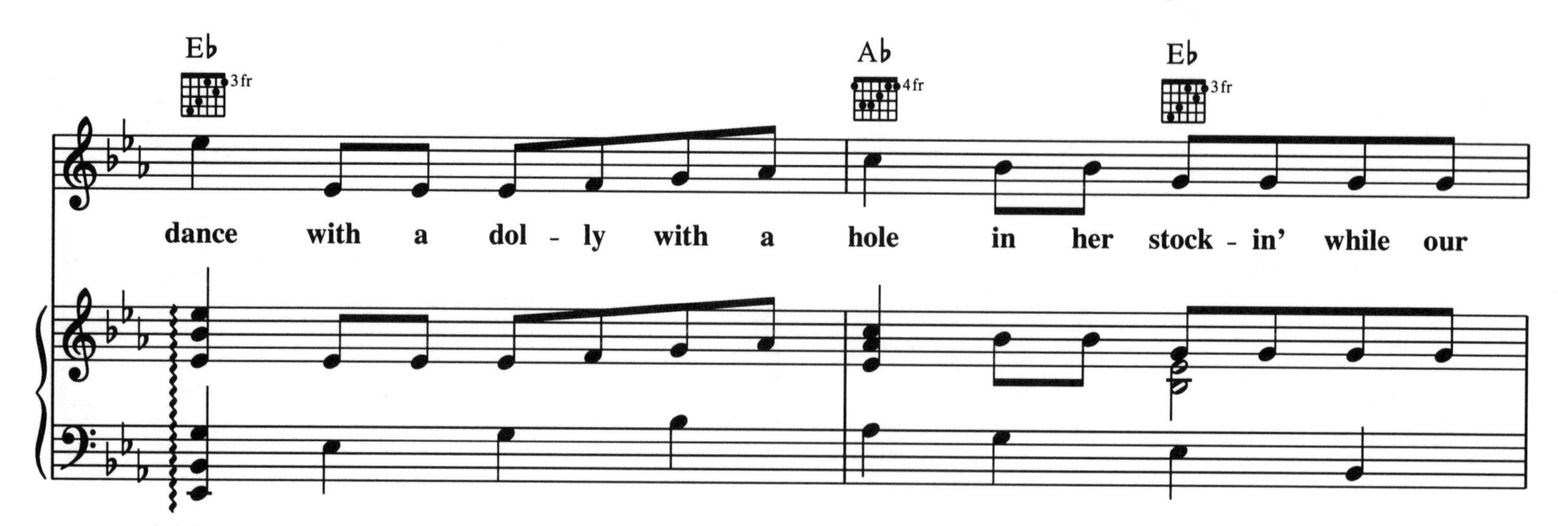
Eb
3fr
Ab
4fr
Eb
3fr
dance with a dol - ly with a hole in her stock - in' while our

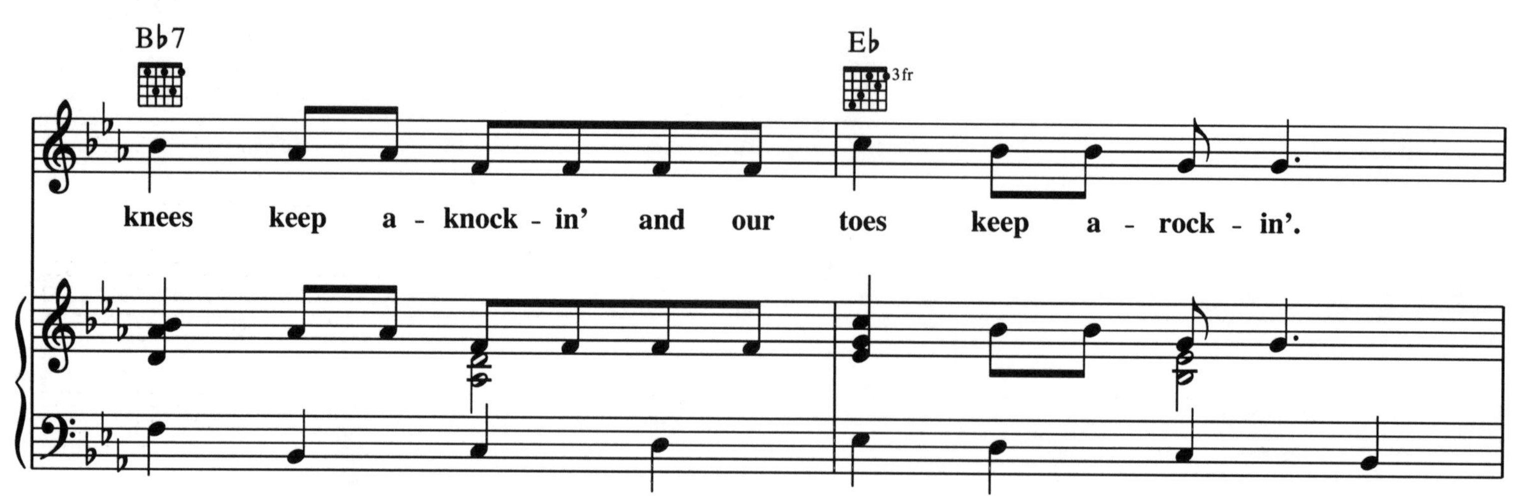
Bb7
Eb
3fr
knees keep a - knock - in' and our toes keep a - rock - in'.

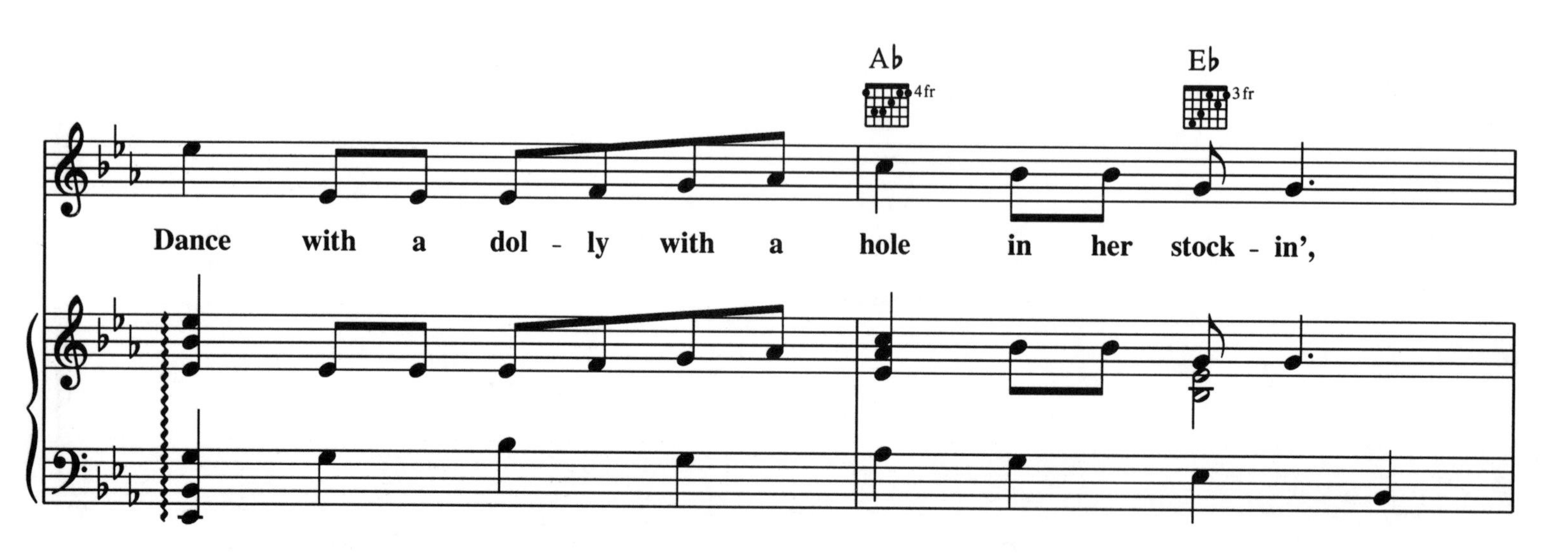
Ab
4fr
Eb
3fr
Dance with a dol - ly with a hole in her stock - in',

B♭7
1,2
E♭
3fr
no chord
dance by the light of the moon. She's
3
B♭7
E♭
Gon-na dance by the light of the moon,
B♭7
E♭
no chord
B♭
Cm7
C♯dim7
dance by the light of the moon, by the light
B♭7/D
B♭7♯5
E♭
A♭m6
4fr
E♭
of the moon.
8vbasso

DANKE SCHOEN

Lyrics by KURT SCHWABACH and MILT GABLER
Music by BERT KAEMPFERT

F+5 F C
— se - cond bal - con - y was the place we'd meet,
— Cen - tral Park in fall how you tore your dress,
G7 C+5 C 1. G7-9 3fr. G7 2. G7-9 3fr. G7
se - cond seat, go Dutch treat, you were sweet. that's not all.
what a mess, I con- fess
D♭+5 D♭ 4fr. A♭7-9 A♭7 4fr.
Dank - e schoen, dar - ling dank - e schoen,
Dank - e schoen, dar - ling dank - e schoen,
A♭7-9 A♭7 4fr. D♭+5 D♭ 4fr.
thank you for walks down Lov - er's Lane.
thank you for see - ing me a - gain.

D♭7-9
D♭7
G♭+5
G♭
I can see hearts carved on a tree let - ters
Tho' we go on our sep - 'rate ways still the
D♭
4fr.
A♭7
To Coda
D♭+5
A♭7-9
D.S. al Coda
in - ter twined for all time. Yours and mine, that was fine.
mem - 'ry stays for al - ways.
CODA
A♭
My heart says dank - e schoen weid - er - sehn,
dank - e schoen.

DOLORES

(From The Paramount Picture "LAS VEGAS NIGHTS")

Words by FRANK LOESSER
Music by LOUIS ALTER

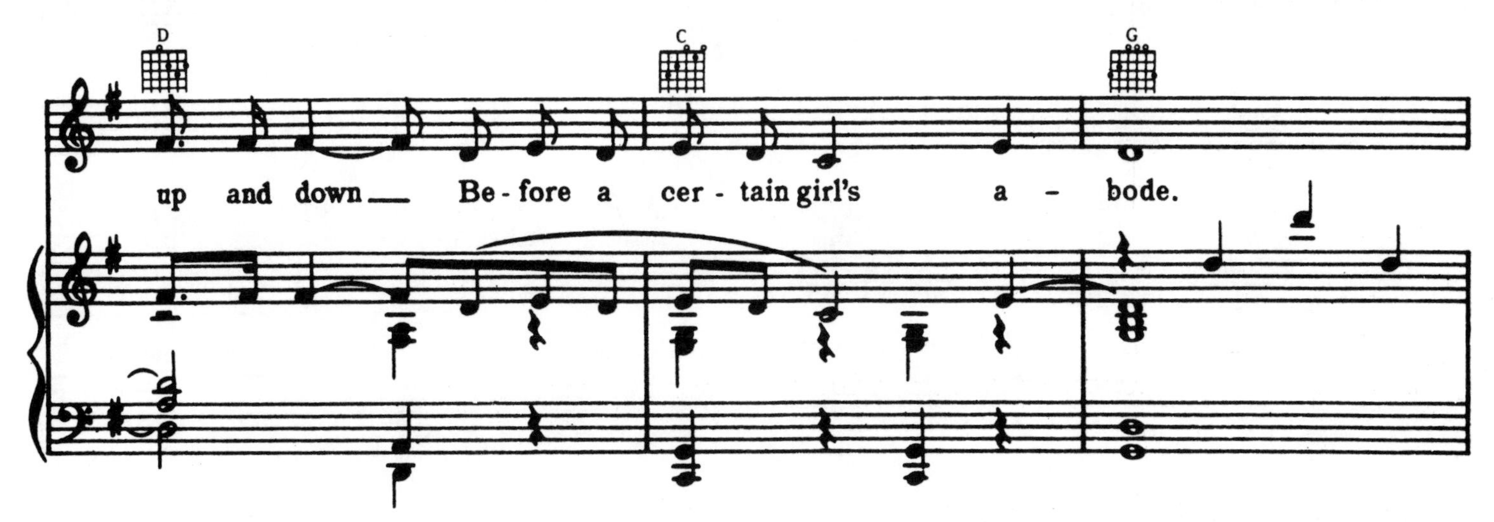

Cm
Cm7
Gm
Cm
D7
F♯dim
Gm
And from a hun-dred lips the mel-o-dy came Croon-ing her name;
rit.
G
Refrain, Molto Moderato (Lightly)
G♯dim
D7
How I love the kiss-es of Do-lo-res Ay, ay, ay, Do-lo-res;
mp - mf
D7sus
D7
Am7
D7
D+
G
Not Ma-rie or Em-i-ly or Dor-is, On-ly my Do-lo-res.
B7
E7
A7
D♯dim
Em
From a bal-co-ny a-bove me, She whis-pers "Love me," and throws a
Bm
F♯m
Bm
Em7
A9
rose, Ah, but she is twice as love-ly as the rose she

D7
C
Fm
D7
G
G♯dim
throws! I would die to be with my Do - lo - res, Ay, ay, ay Do-
D7
D7sus
D7
Am7
D7
D+
lo - res; I was made to ser - e - nade Do - lo - res, Cho - rus af - ter
G
B7
E7
A7
D♯dim
cho - rus. Just im - ag - ine eyes like moon - rise A voice like
Em
G
mu - sic, and lips like wine! What a break if I could make Do-
E7
E7+
E7
A7
D7
1. G
Am7
F♯dim
2. G
lo - res, Mine all mine. mine.

A FINE ROMANCE

(From "SWING TIME")

Words by DOROTHY FIELDS
Music by JEROME KERN

C/E
E♭dim7
Dm7
G7
Dm7
G7
cou - ple of hot to - ma - toes, but
seals in the Arc - tic O - cean, at
C
E7
you're as cold as yes - ter - day's mashed po - ta - toes.
least they flap their fins to ex - press e - mo - tion.
Dm7
G7
C
C♯dim7
G7
A fine ro - mance! You won't
A fine ro - mance! With no
G7♯5
C
G7
nest - le; a fine ro - mance, you won't
quar - els, with no in - sults, and all

C
A7
wrest - le! I might as well play bridge with my old maid
mor - als! I've nev - er mussed the crease in your blue serge
Dm
A7/E
F
F#dim7
C/G
aunts! I have - n't got a chance.
pants, I nev - er get the chance.
G7
C
Dm7
G7
This is a fine ro - mance!
This is a fine ro -
C
Dm7
G7
C
G7
(She:) A mance!

C
Dm7/G
G7
C
B7
G7
Dm7/G
G7
C
(He:) A fine ro - mance! With no kiss - es! A fine ro - mance, my friend, this is! We two should be like
fine ro - mance! My dear Duch - ess! Two old fo - gies who need crutch - es! True love should have the
G7
G7#5
C
G7
C

C/E
E♭dim
Dm7
G7
Dm7
G7
clams in a dish of chow - der. But
thrills that a health - y crime has! We
C
E7
we just "fizz" like parts of a Seid - litz pow - der.
don't have half the thrills that the "March of Time" has!
Dm7
G7
C
C♯dim7
G7
A fine ro - mance with no
A fine ro - mance, my good
G7♯5
C
G7
clinch - es. A fine ro - mance with no
wom - an! My strong "Aged in the wood"

C
A7
pinch - es. You're just as hard to land as the "Ile de
wom - an! You nev er give the or - chids I send a
Dm
A7/E
F
F#dim7
C/G
France!" I have - n't got a chance,
glance! No! You like cac - tus plants,
G7
1
C
Dm7
G7
this is a fine ro - mance!
this is a fine ro -
mf
C
Dm7
G7
2
C
(He:) A mance!
sfz

THE GIRL THAT I MARRY

(From The Stage Production "ANNIE GET YOUR GUN")

Words and Music by
IRVING BERLIN

F7
B♭
B♭/F
pink as a nurs - er - y. The
girl I call my own
will wear sat - ins and lac - es and
C7/E
F7/E♭
B♭/D
Cm/E♭
smell of col - ogne. Her nails will be pol - ished and

Cm7
F7
F7/C
F7
in her hair, she'll wear a gar - den - ia. And
B♭
B♭9
I'll be there, 'stead of flit - tin' I'll be
E♭
sit - tin' next to her and she'll
Edim7
B♭/F
Fdim
F7
F9
purr like a kit - ten. A

B♭
B♭/F
Bdim
F7/C
F7
Gm7/F
doll I can car - ry, the girl that I
F7
E♭/F
F7
1
B♭/D
Cm7/E♭
mar - ry must be.
F7
B♭
2
B♭/D
The
be.
Cm7/E♭
F7
B♭

GLAD TO BE UNHAPPY
(From "ON YOUR TOES")

Words by LORENZ HART
Music by RICHARD RODGERS

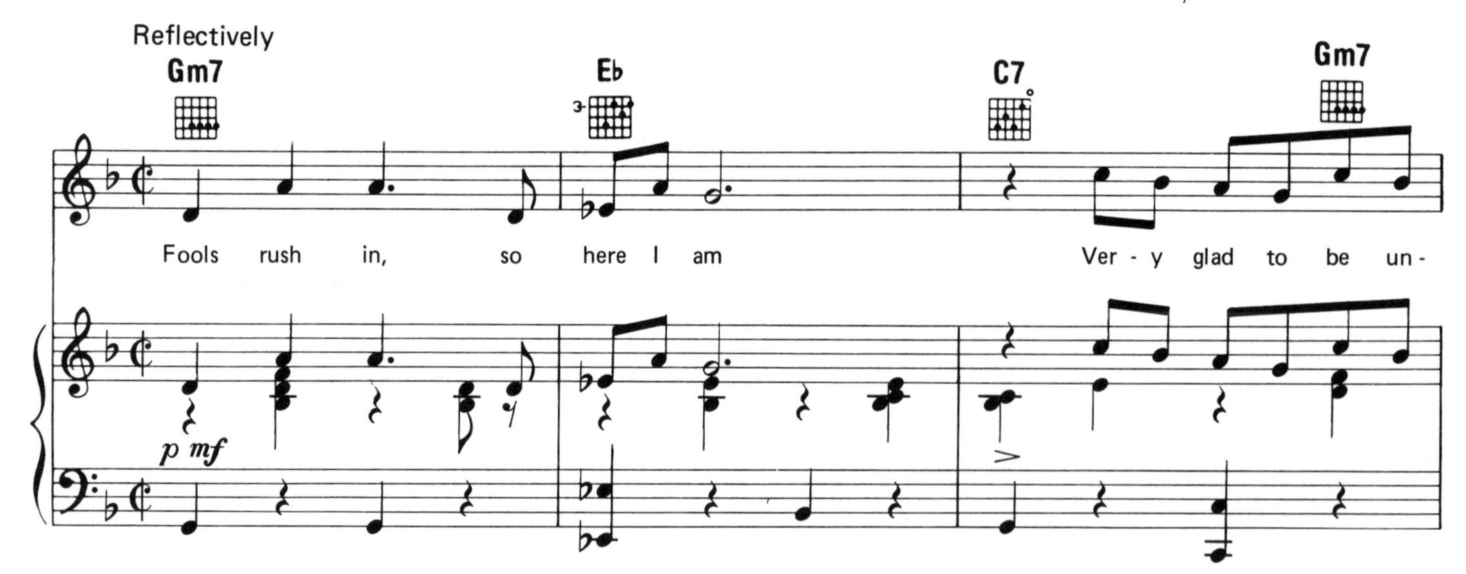

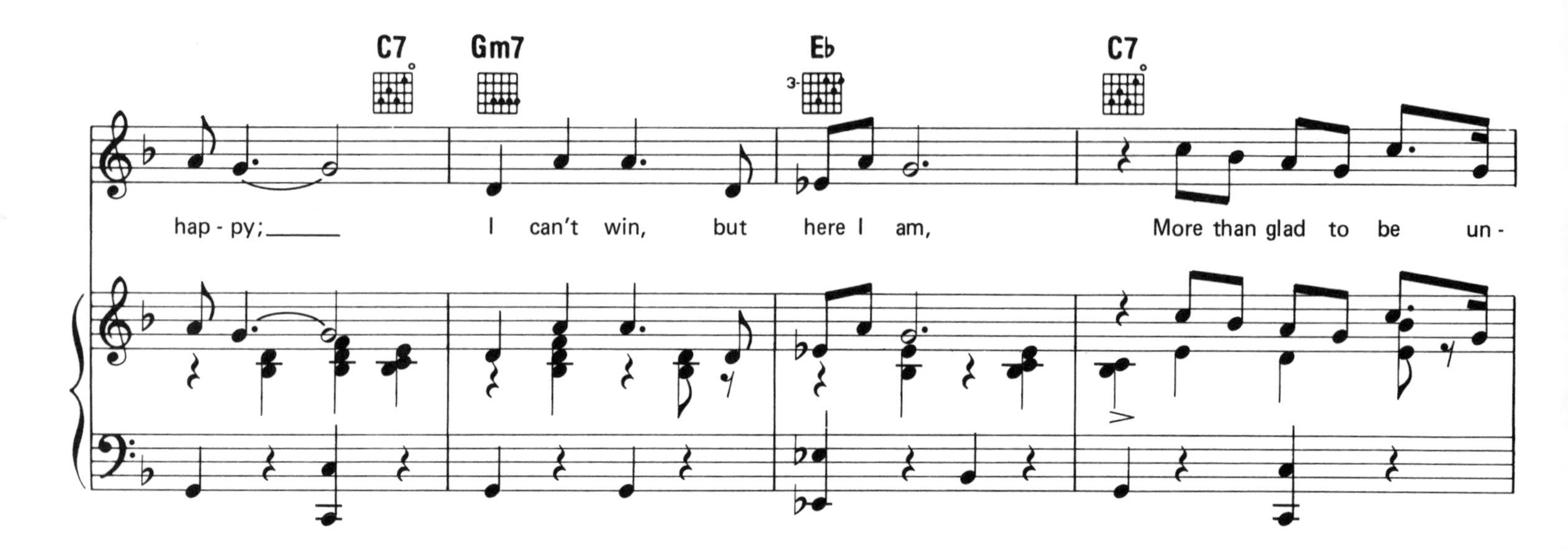

F
Bb
G#dim
F
bad,
But for some one you a - dore,
mf
Gm7
C7
F
Gm7
Eb
It's a pleas-ure to be sad.
Like a stray - ing ba-by lamb,
p
C7
Gm7
C7
F
Dm
Gm7
C9
With no mam-my and no pap-py,
I'm so un - hap-py,
But oh, so
glad!
glad!
mf
mp

THE GLORY OF LOVE

Words and Music by
BILLY HILL

G D7 G Gmaj7 G7 C
laugh a lit-tle, cry a lit-tle be-fore the clouds roll by a lit-tle
G D7 G C Cm
that's the sto - ry of, that's the glo - ry of love.
D7 G7 C
As long as there's the two of us we've got the
G C7 Gdim7 G D7 G G7 Cm
world and all its charms and when the world is

Gdim7 G7 Cdim A7
Am7
D7
through with us
we've got each oth - ers arms.
You've got to
G
D7
G
Gmaj7
G7
win a lit - tle, lose a lit - tle
and al - ways have the
C
G
D7
blues a lit - tle
that's the sto - ry of,
that's the glo - ry of
1
G
G♯dim7
Am7
D9
4
love.
You've got to
2
G
Cm6
2
Gmaj7
love.

HARLEM NOCTURNE

Words by DICK ROGERS
Music by EARLE HAGEN

Gm(maj7)
Cm6
a noc-turne born in Har - lem that mel-an-cho-ly strain
Cm(maj7)
E♭
E♭7
D7
Gm
C9
for-ev - er is haunt-ing me.
Gm
G♭9♯5
F9
B♭7
Fm7
B♭7
Fm7
The mel - o - dy clings a - round my heart strings. It
In-di-go tune it sings to the moon the
B♭7
Fm7
B♭7
B7
B♭7
E♭7
B♭m7
won't let me go when I'm lone - ly. I hear it in dreams and
lone-some re-frain of a lov - er. The mel - o - dy sighs it

E♭7
B♭m7
no chord
1
F7
some-how it seems
it makes me weep and I can't sleep. An
laughs and it cries
a moon in blue that
2
Gm
D7♯5
Gm
no chord
Gm(maj7)
wails the long night thru.
Tho' with the dawn it's gone
Cm6
Cm(maj7)
the mel-o-dy lives ev - er
for lone-ly hearts to learn
E♭
E♭7
D7
Gm
D7
Gm
C13
Gm
of love in a Har-lem Noc-turne.

HEART AND SOUL

(From The Paramount Short Subject "A SONG IS BORN")

Words by FRANK LOESSER
Music by HOAGY CARMICHAEL

Moderately, not too fast

F Dm7 Gm7 C7 Dm7 G9

mf

C9sus Gm7/C F F♯dim7

ad lib. *mp*

I've let a pair of arms en - slave me oft

Gm C7 F6 Gm7/C

times be - fore, but more than just a thrill you

F G7 Gm7/C C7

gave me, yes more, much more.

Moderately, lightly rhythmical
F Dm7 Gm7 C7 F Dm7
Heart and soul I fell in love with you. Heart and soul
mp
Gm7 C7 F Dm Gm C7
the way a fool would do, mad - ly be-cause you held me
mf
F Dm7 Gm7 C7 F Dm7
tight and stole a kiss in the night. Heart and soul
Gm7 C7 F Dm7 Gm7 C7
I begged to be a-dored. Lost con - trol and tum-bled o - ver-board,

F
Dm
Gm
C7
F
glad - ly that mag - ic night we kissed there in the
F7
B♭
A7
D7
G7
moon - mist. Oh! but your lips were thrill - ing,
mf
C7
F7
E7
A7
B♭
A7
much too thrill - ing. Nev - er be - fore were
D7
G7
C7
F7
E7
C7
mine so strange - ly will - ing. But

F Dm7 Gm7 C7 F Dm7
now I see what one em-brace can do. Look at me,
Gm7 C7 F Dm Gm7 C7
it's got me lov-ing you mad - ly, that lit-tle kiss you
A7 D7 Gm G9 C7 1 F Dm7
stole held all my heart and soul.
Gm7 C7 2 F Dm7 Gm7 C7♭9 F
soul.

I DON'T WANT TO WALK WITHOUT YOU

Words by FRANK LOESSER
Music by JULE STYNE

Fm
F7
I don't want to walk with - out you, ba -
B♭7
E♭
3fr
by, walk with-out my arm a - bout you,
Gm7♭5
5fr
C7
F9
ba - by. I thought the
Fm7
B♭7
E♭
3fr
day you left me be - hind,

Gm
A7
D7
Gm
E♭m/G♭
I'd take a stroll and get you right off my mind, but
F7
B♭7
Edim7
Fm
now I find that I don't want to walk with - out the
F7
B♭7
E♭
sun - shine. Why'd you have to
Gm7♭5
C7
turn off all that sun - shine?

F9 Fm7 B♭7
Oh, ba - by please come back ___ or you'll
E♭ B♭7/F E♭/G F♯dim7 Gm7 C9
break my heart for me, 'cause
Fm
I ___ don't want to walk with - out you,
Fm7/B♭ B♭7 1 E♭6 B♭7 B♭7♯5(♭9) 2 E♭ E♭6
no - sir - ee. ee.

I GET ALONG WITHOUT YOU VERY WELL
(EXCEPT SOMETIMES)

Words and Music by
HOAGY CARMICHAEL
Inspired by a poem written by J.B.

F7 Cm7 E♭m6 B♭
call the thrill of be - ing shel - tered in your arms,
B♭/D D♭dim7 Cm7 F7 Cm7
Of course I do, But I get a - long with -
E♭m/F B♭ Gm7 Cm7 F7 B♭6
out you ver - y well. I've for - got - ten
Cm7 Cm7/F F7 B♭ B♭/D D♭dim7 Cm7
you, just like I should, Of course I have,

F7
Cm7
3fr
F7
Except to hear your name or some-one's
Cm7
3fr
F7
laugh that is the same But I've for-got-ten
B♭
E♭/B♭
6fr
B♭
B♭7
E♭
3fr
you just like I should What a guy!
E♭dim7
B♭
Gm7
3fr
Cm
3fr
What a fool am I To think my break-ing heart

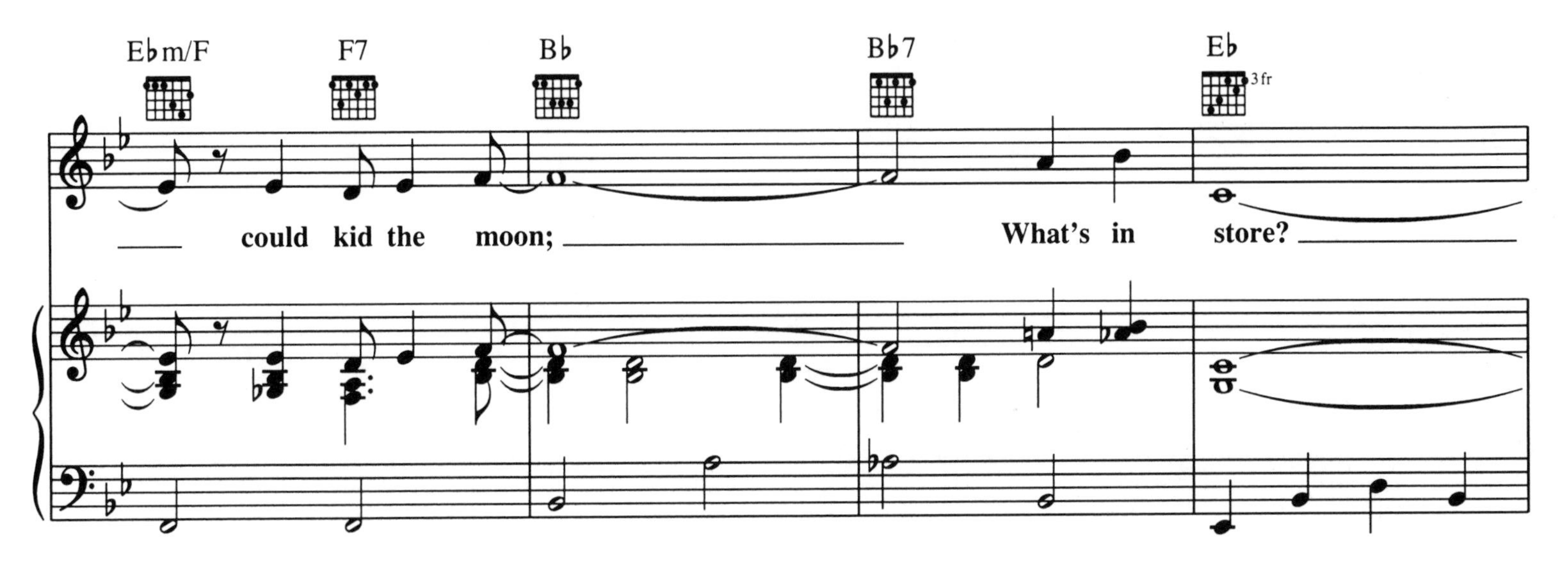
E♭m/F
F7
B♭
B♭7
E♭
3fr
could kid the moon;
What's in store?

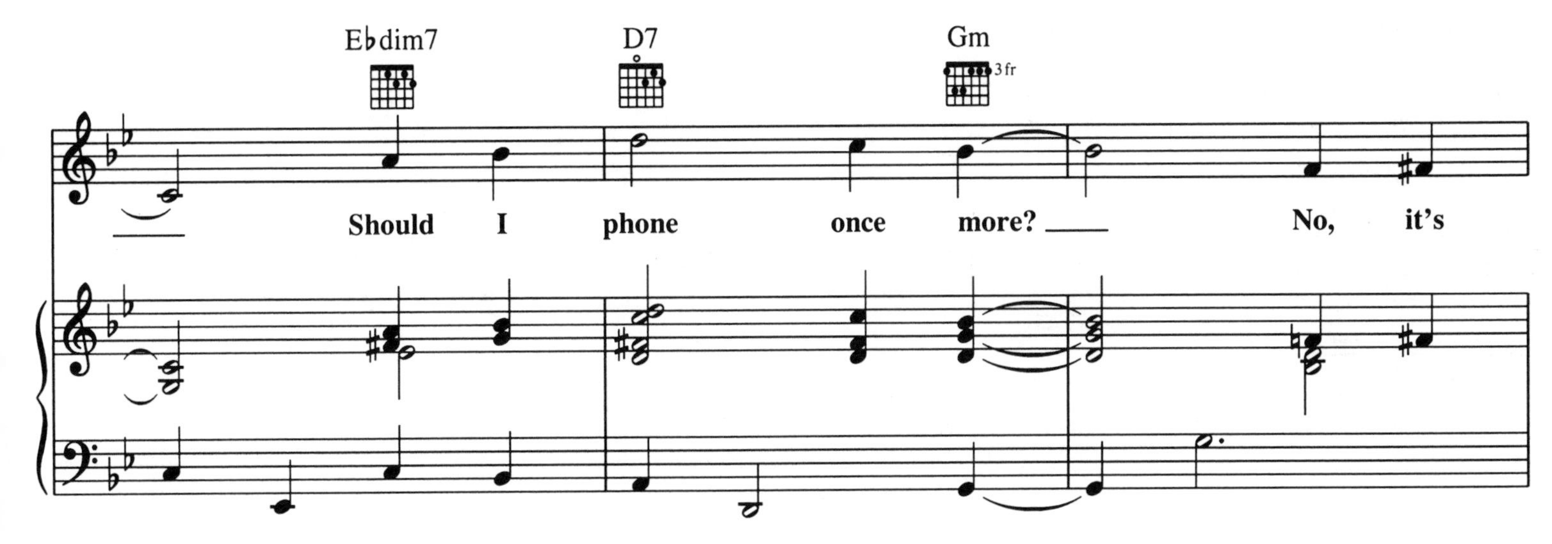
E♭dim7
D7
Gm
3fr
Should I phone once more?
No, it's

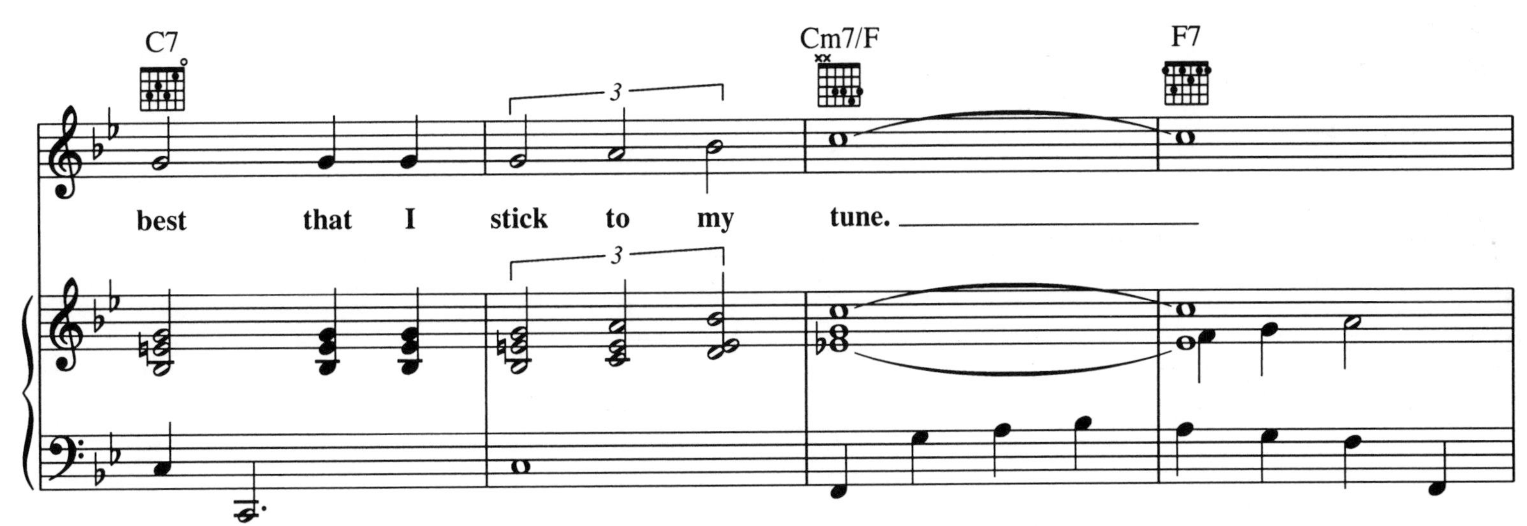
C7
Cm7/F
F7
3
best that I stick to my tune.

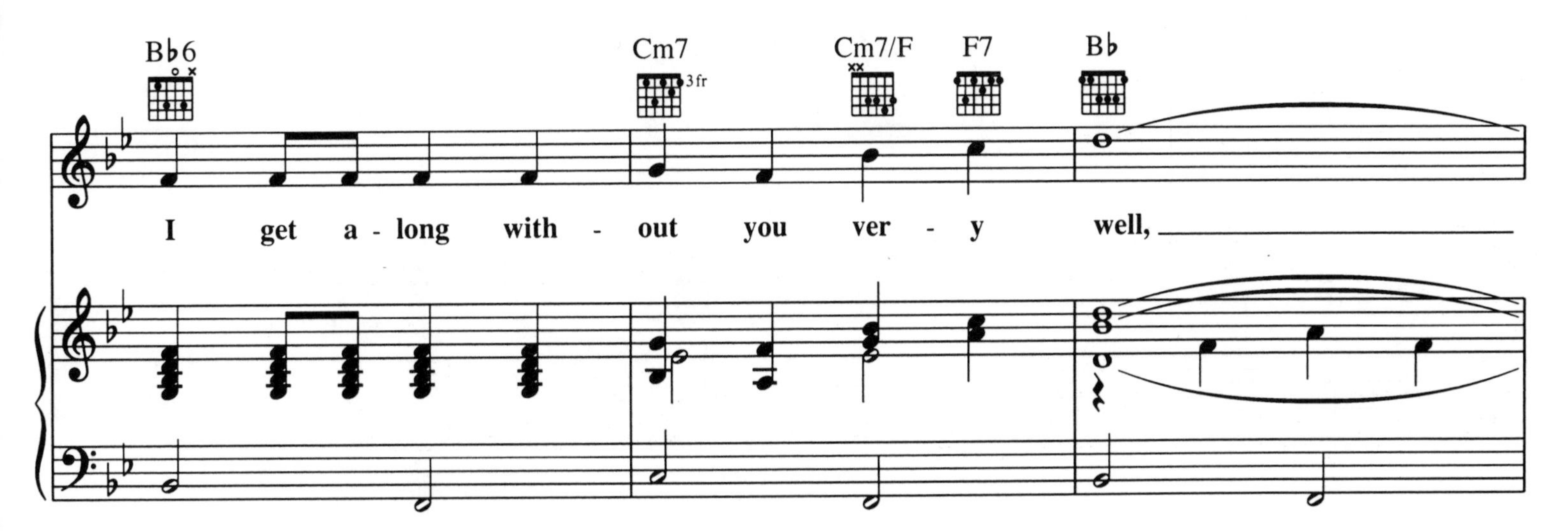
B♭6
Cm7
3fr
Cm7/F
F7
B♭
I get a - long with - out you ver - y well,

B♭/D D♭dim7 Cm7 F7
Of course I do, Except per -
Cm7 F7 Cm7
haps in spring but I should nev - er think of
F7 Cm Ebm6
spring For that would sure - ly break my heart in
1 B♭ B♭/D D♭dim7 Cm7 F7
two.
2 B♭
two.
rit.
3 fr

I LEFT MY HEART IN SAN FRANCISCO

Words by DOUGLAS CROSS
Music by GEORGE CORY

D7♭9
Gm
Gm(maj7)
C9sus
that was Rome is of an - oth - er day.
C9
F9sus
Freely
F9
Cm7♭5
I've been ter - ri - bly a - lone and for - got - ten in Man - hat - tan.
rit.
Gm7♭5
G♭9
With a slow, steady beat
F/C
I'm go - ing home to my cit - y by the bay.
D7/C
C9sus
C9
F9sus
Fdim7

F9
Cm7
C♯dim7
B♭maj9
C♯dim7
I left my heart in San Fran -
Cm7
F9sus
cis - co.
High on a hill,
F7
B♭maj7
Cm7
B♭maj7
Cm7
C♯dim7
it calls to me.
To be where
B♭maj7
B♭m6
Am/C
lit - tle ca-ble cars
climb half-way to the stars!

Am7
D7♭9
4fr
Gm7
3fr
C9
C7♭9
— The morn - ing fog may chill the
F9sus
F9
Bdim7
Cm7
3fr
F7
C♯dim7
B♭maj9
air; I don't care! My love waits there
C♯dim7
Cm7
3fr
in San Fran - cis - co, a - bove the
F9
E♭6/G
3fr
F7/A
3fr
E♭/G
3fr
E♭6
D
C/E
blue and wind - y sea.

D7/F♯
D7
G7♯5
G9
F/A
G7/B
When I come home to you, San Fran -
C9sus
Gm7
C9
B9
C9
F9sus
cis - co, your gold - en sun will
Cm7
F7♭5(♭9)
1
B♭6
A♭13
B♭6/9
Cm7
C♯dim7
shine for me! I left my
2
B♭6
A♭13
B♭6/9
G♭maj7
B♭6/9
me!
dim. e rit.

I GOT LOST IN HIS ARMS

Words and Music by
IRVING BERLIN

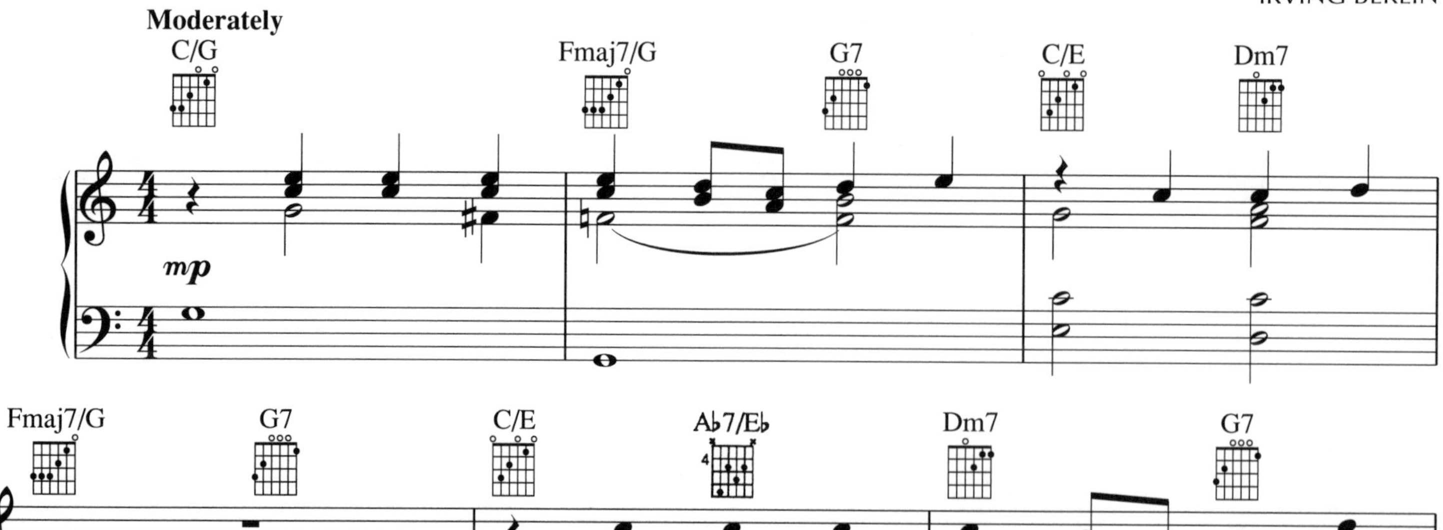

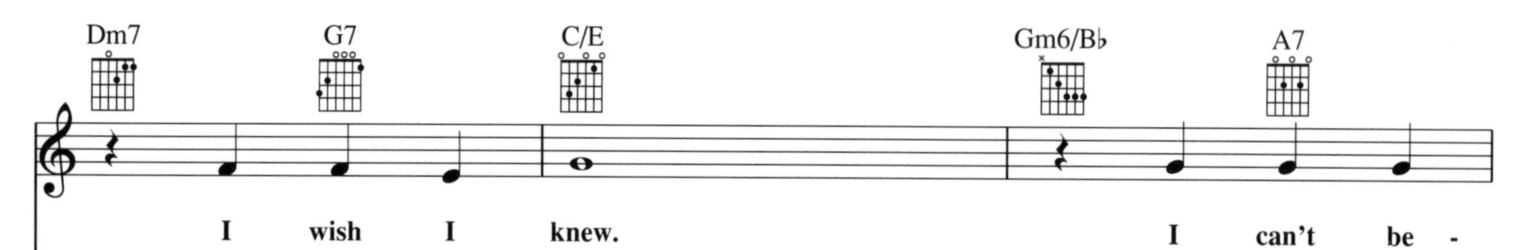

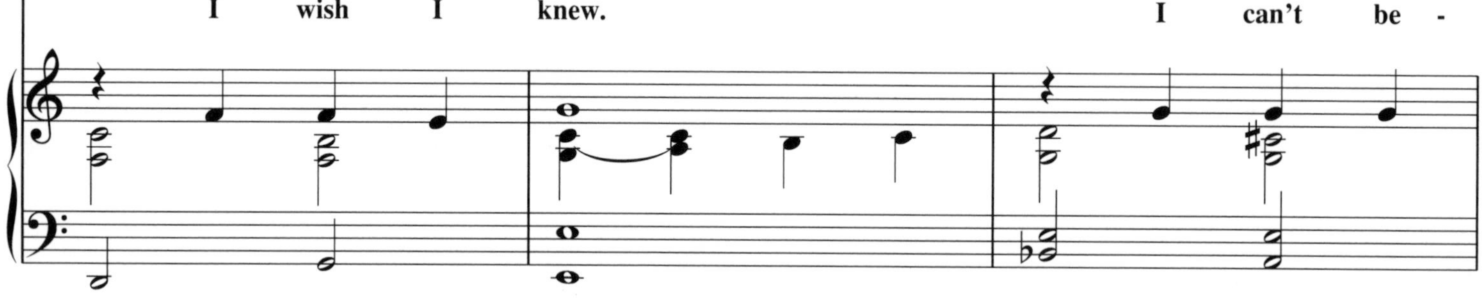

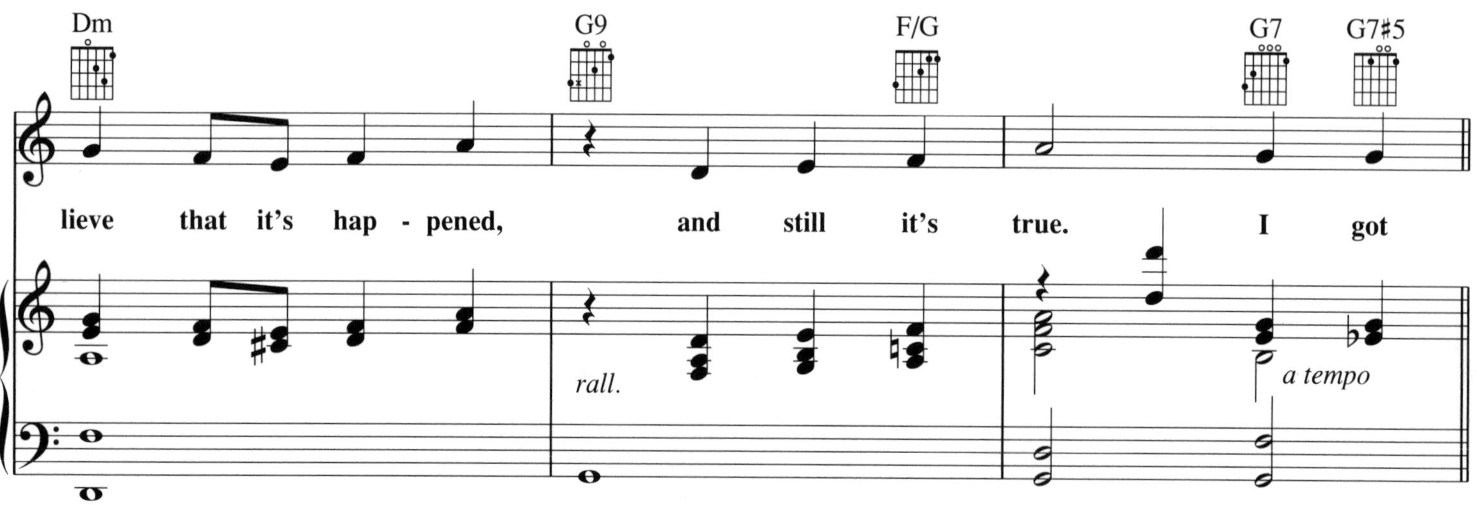

C(add9)
C
Cmaj7
C6
lost in his arms, and I had to stay.
A7♯5
Dm(add9)
Dm
It was dark in his arms, and I
Dm7
D♭7
C7
Gm11
lost my way.
From the dark came a
F♯dim
Fm7
C6/E
Am/G
voice, and it seemed to say,
"There you

Dm7
Gdim7
Dm7/G
Fm6/G
go. There you go."
G7
G7#5
C(add9)
C
How I felt as I fell I just
Cmaj7
C6
A7#5
Dm(add9)
can't re - call. But his arms held me
Dm
Dm7
D♭7
C7
fast, and it broke the fall. And I

Gm11
Fmaj7
Fm6
said to my heart as it fool - ish - ly kept
C/E
E♭dim7
Dm7
G7
A7♯5♭9
A7♭9
jump - ing all a - round,
"I got
Dm7
G7
F/G
G7sus(♭9)
C6
1
Em7
lost but look what I found."
rall.
a tempo
Dm7
G7
G7♯5
2 C
Fmaj7
C6/9
I got

I WISH I DIDN'T LOVE YOU SO

(From The Paramount Picture "THE PERILS OF PAULINE")

Words and Music by
FRANK LOESSER

E♭ E♭7 A♭ A♭m E♭ Cm
kiss, Why must your kiss
F9 Fm7/B♭ E♭ A♭m E♭ no chord
tor-ture me as long as this? I might be
C7♯5(♭9) C7 C7♭9 Fm
smil - ing by now with some new ten - der friend,
G7♭9 D♭7 C7 C7♭5 Cm9
Smil - ing by now with my heart

Cm7/F
F9
Fm7
E7
E♭
Cm
on the mend. But when I try,
Gm
Fm
B♭7♭9
E♭
E♭7
A♭
A♭m
Some-thing in that heart says "No," You're still there,
E♭
Cm
F9
Fm7/B♭
1
E♭
Cm
I wish I did-n't love you so.
Fm7
E7
2
E♭
A♭m
E♭
E♭maj7

IN THE COOL, COOL, COOL OF THE EVENING

(From The Paramount Picture "HERE COMES THE GROOM")

Words by JOHNNY MERCER
Music by HOAGY CARMICHAEL

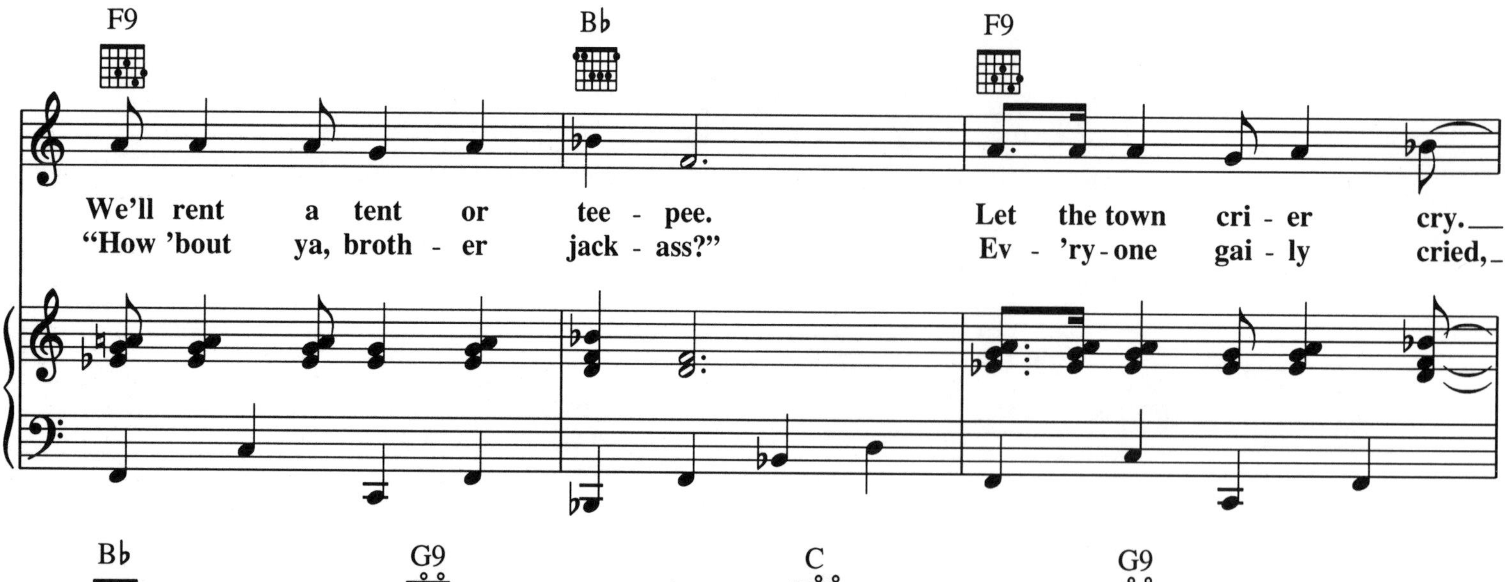
F9
B♭
F9
We'll rent a tent or tee - pee.
Let the town cri - er cry.
"How 'bout ya, broth - er jack - ass?"
Ev - 'ry - one gai - ly cried,

B♭
G9
C
G9
And if it's R. S. V. P.
this is what I'll re -
"You com - in' to the fra - cas?"
O - ver his specks he

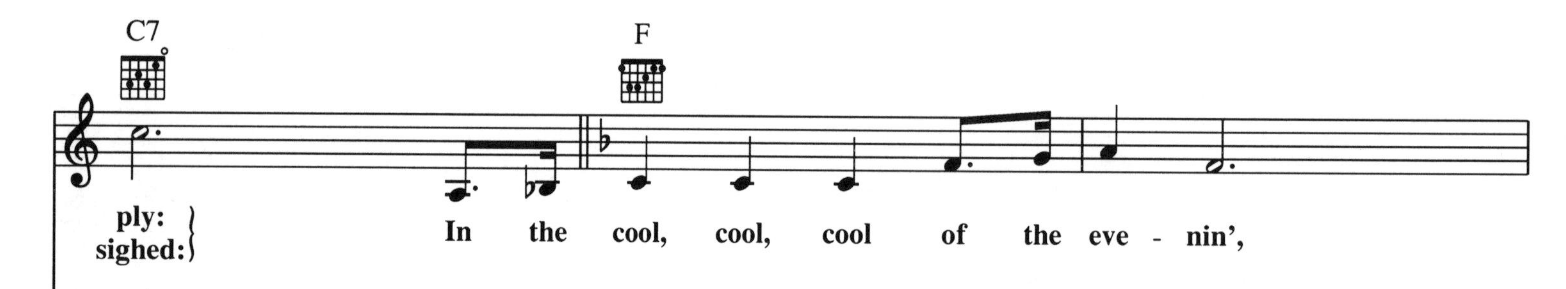
C7
F
ply:
sighed:
In the cool, cool, cool of the eve - nin',

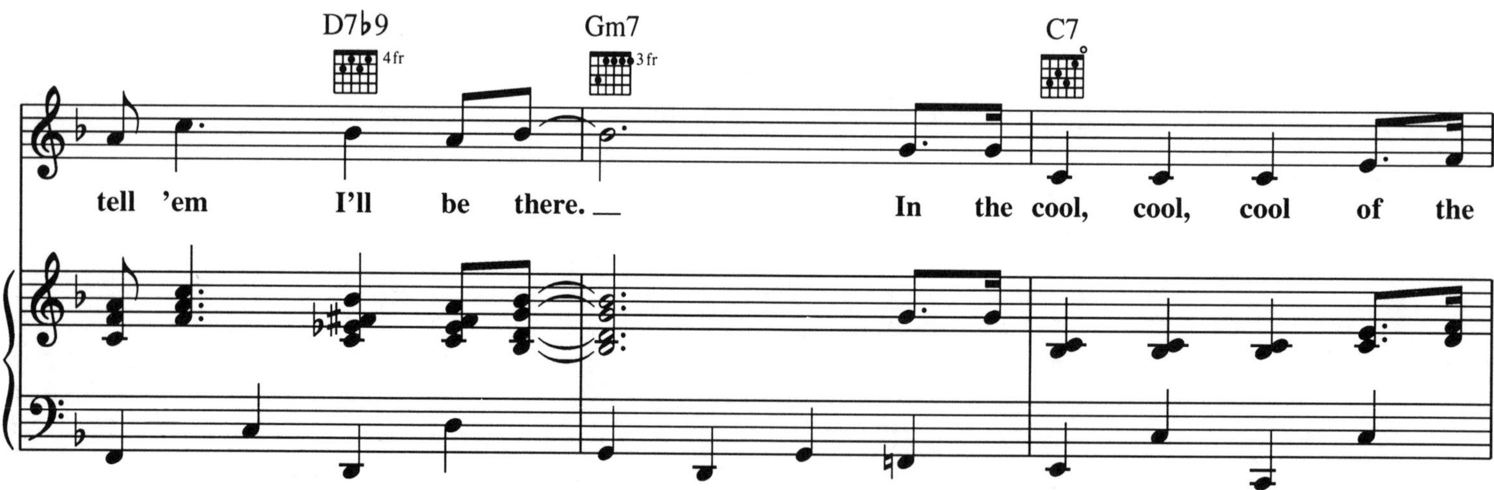
D7♭9
4fr
Gm7
3fr
C7
tell 'em I'll be there.
In the cool, cool, cool of the

C7♭9
F
C7
eve - nin',
bet - ter save a chair.
slick - um on my hair.
When the
F
Cm7
3fr
F7
par - ty's get - tin' a glow on, 'n' sing - in' fills the air,
B♭
B♭m6
6fr
F/C
E♭6
D7
in the shank o' the night, when the do - in's are right, you can
if I ain't in the clink, and there's sump - in' to drink, you can
Gm
3fr
C7
1
F
B♭7
A7
2
F
tell 'em I'll be there.
tell 'em I'll be there.

I WISH I WERE IN LOVE AGAIN

(From "BABES IN ARMS")

Words by LORENZ HART
Music by RICHARD RODGERS

Am7 D7 G Em7 A7 D7
sleep all night, Ap - pe - tite and health re - stored.
G C A7 D7 G#dim D7
You don't know how much I'm bored!
G A#dim G
The sleep - less nights, The dai - ly fights, The quick to - bog - gan when you
fur - tive sigh, The black - ened eye, The words "I'll love you till the
p-mf
A#dim G A#dim
reach the heigths; I miss the kiss - es and I miss the bites, I
day I die," The self - de - cep - tion that be - lieves the lie, I

D7
C#dim
D7
D7sus
G
A#dim
wish I were in love a-gain! The bro-ken dates, The end-less waits, The
wish I were in love a-gain! When love con-geals It soon re-veals The
G
A#dim
G
love-ly lov-ing and the hate-ful hates, The con-ver-sa-tion with the
faint a-rom-a of per-form-ing seals, The dou-ble cross-ing of a
A#dim
D7
G7
fly-ing plates, I wish I were in love a-gain!
pair of heels I wish I were in love a-gain!
C
Cm
G
E+
A7
D7
G
G7
No more pain, No more strain,
No more care, No de-spair.
mf

C Cm G E+ A7
Now___ I'm sane, but___ I would rath - er be
I'm___ all there now,___ But I'd rath - er be
D7 G A♯dim
ga - ga!___ The pulled out fur of cat and cur, The
punch - drunk!___ Be - lieve me sir, I much pre - fer The
p
G A♯dim G
fine mis - mat - ing of a him and her, I've learned my les - son, but I
clas - sic bat - tle of a him and her, I don't like qui - et and I
B7 Em Am7 D7 1 G Am7 D7 2 G Am7 G
wish I were in love a - gain! The
wish I were in love a - gain!
mf
sf

IN THE MOOD

Words and Music by
JOE GARLAND

G
D7
Hope she tells me may - be, what a wing it will be
So, I said po - lite - ly "Dar - lin'

Am7
G
C6
Eb7
D7
G6
may I in - trude" She said "Don't keep me wait - in' when I'm In The Mood"

G
First I held her light - ly and we start - ed to dance
Then I held her tight - ly what a

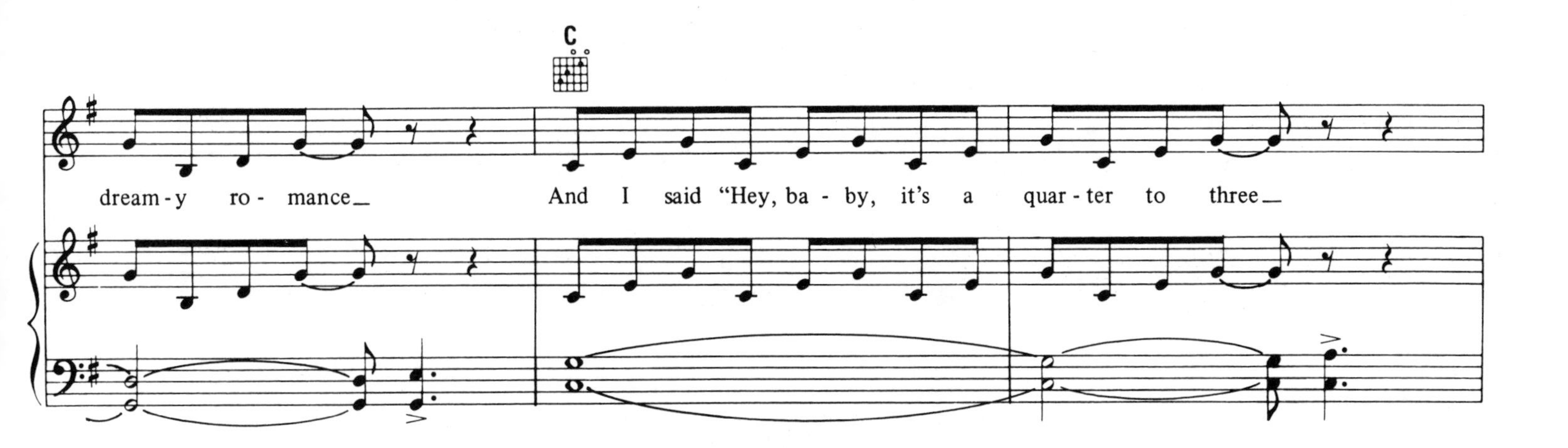
C
dream - y ro - mance
And I said "Hey, ba - by, it's a quar - ter to three

G
D7
There's a mess of moon-light won't-cha share it with me"
"Well" she ans-wered "Mis-ter, don't-cha

Am7
G
C6
Eb
D11
G6
Fine
know that it's rude To keep my two lips wait-in' when they're In The Mood!"

G
Gdim
Am7
D7-9
G
Gdim
In The Mood That's what she told me In The Mood

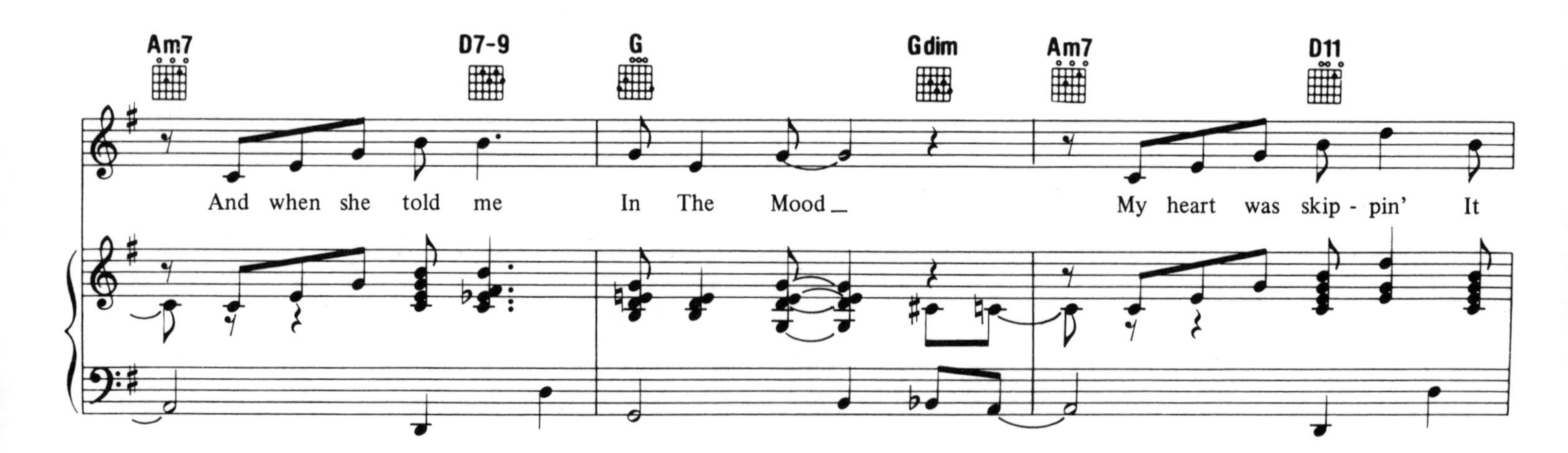
Am7
D7-9
G
Gdim
Am7
D11
And when she told me In The Mood My heart was skip-pin' It

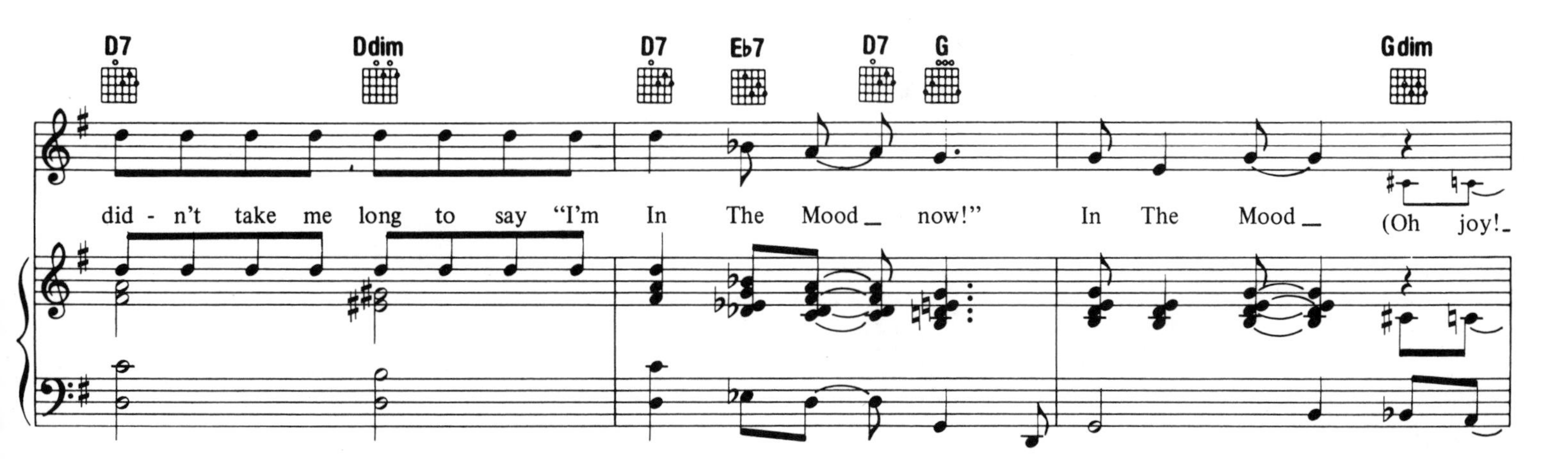
D7
Ddim
D7
Eb7
D7
G
Gdim
did - n't take me long to say "I'm In The Mood_ now!" In The Mood_ (Oh joy!_

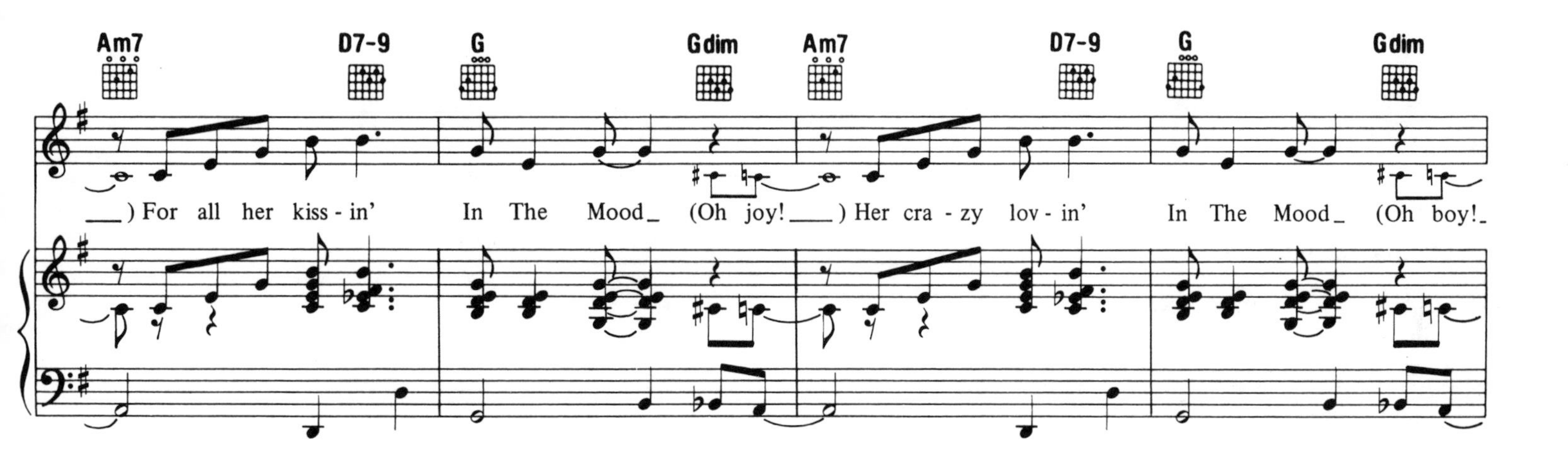
Am7
D7-9
G
Gdim
Am7
D7-9
G
Gdim
___) For all her kiss - in' In The Mood_ (Oh joy!___) Her cra - zy lov - in' In The Mood_ (Oh boy!_

Am7
D11
D7
Ddim
1 D7
Eb7
D7
G
2 D7
Eb7
D7
G
___) What I was miss - in' It did - n't take me long to say I'm In The Mood_ now. In The Mood_ now.

Tacet
D.S. al Fine

IN THE WEE SMALL HOURS OF THE MORNING

Words by BOB HILLIARD
Music by DAVID MANN

C
D♭7
4fr
C
wee small hours of the morn - in', there's just the
D♭7
4fr
C
C7
F7
pian-o play-er and me. He's play - in' songs I sang with
C
C♯dim7
Dm7
E♭m6
Dm7
G7
ba - by, and I cling to that sweet mem - o -
C6
Fm7
B♭9
E♭maj7
3fr
Gm7
3fr
G♭m7
ry. Oh! what times we had to - geth - er;

Fm7
B♭7
E♭
3fr
man - y a laugh and not a care.
Dm7♭5
G7
Cm7
F7
Come to think a - bout it, that tells the sto - ry, The
Am7♭5
A♭7♭5
G7
G7#5
sto - ry of the whole af - fair.
In the
C
D♭7
4fr
C
wee small hours of the morn - in', it gets too

D♭7 C C7 F7
strong for the likes of me. I get to long - in' for my
C C♯dim7 Dm7 F E7
ba - by, and an - y fool can plain - ly
Am D7 F7 C7♭9 F7 Am7
see that the wee small hours of the morn - in' are just a
Dm7 G13 G13♭9 C6 A♭9 G7 G7♯5 C6 D♭6/9 C6/9
mis - er - y to me. In the me.

INDIAN LOVE CALL

(From "ROSE-MARIE")

Lyrics by OTTO HARBACH and OSCAR HAMMERSTEIN II
Music by RUDOLF FRIML

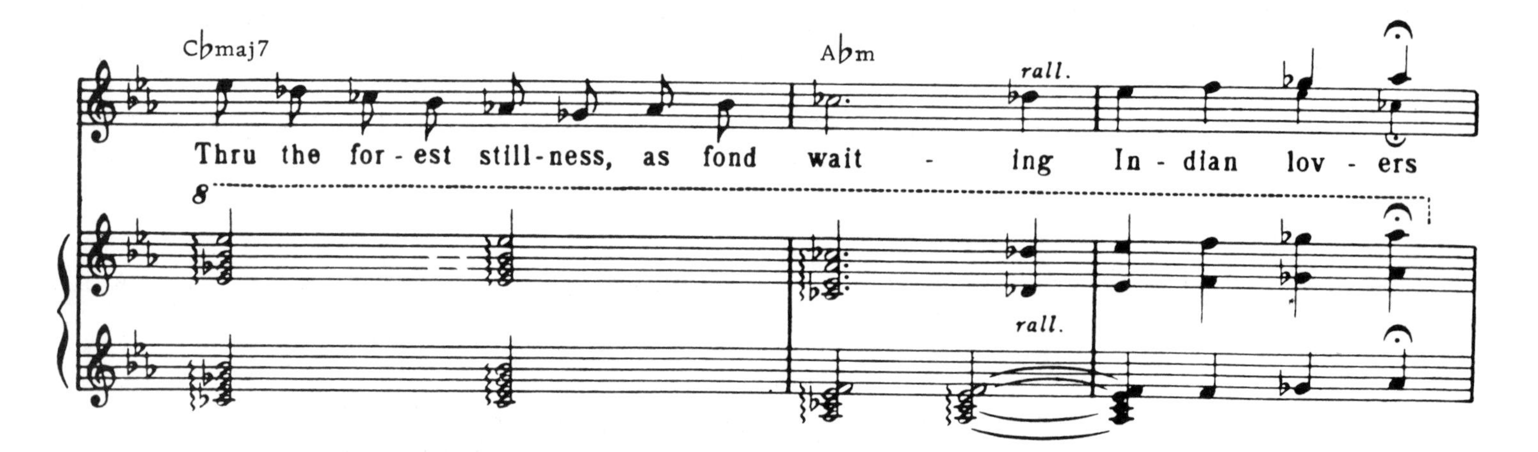

B♭
A♭
G♭
B♭7
call!
p poco accel.
sostenuto
mf
rit.
p
Moderato
E♭m
E♭
p
When the lone la - goon Stirs in the Spring, Wel-com-ing

p

G♭+
E♭+
E♭m
ten.
home some swan-y white wing, When the maid-en moon, Rid-ing the

E♭m
G♭+
E♭+
ten.
sky, gath-ers her star - eyed dream chil-dren nigh:

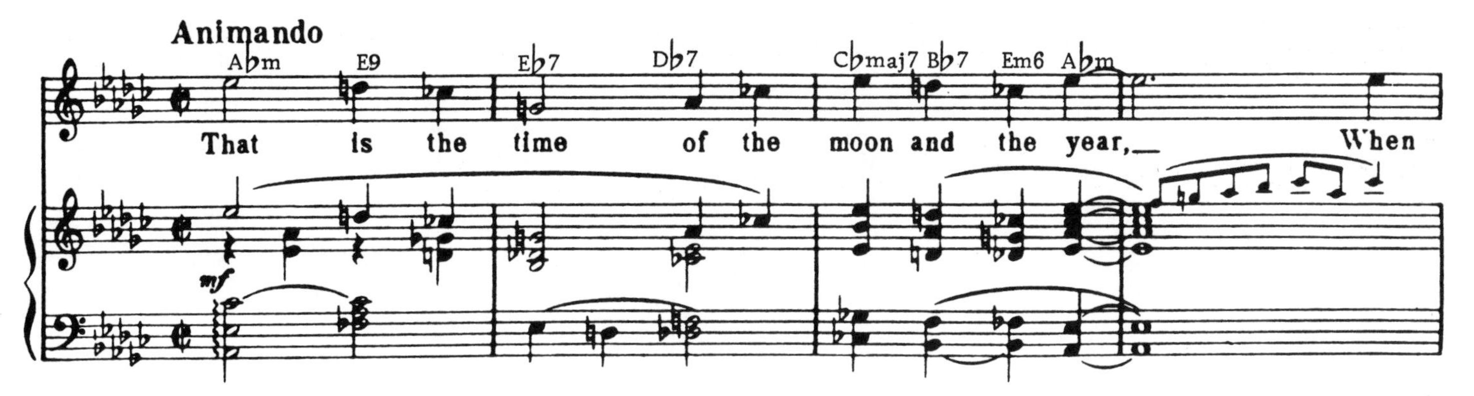

Animando
A♭m
E9
E♭7
D♭7
C♭maj7
B♭7
Em6
A♭m
That is the time of the moon and the year, When
mf

G♭ G7 G♭ G7 G♭7 E♭9
love - dreams to In - di - an maid - ens ap - pear. And
E7 E9♭5 E+ G♭+ C7+5 B♭
this is the song that they hear: When I'm call - ing
p
pp
p
REFRAIN (Slowly)
Fm6 B♭ E♭
you oo - oo oo - oo - oo! Will you an - swer
molto espr.
pp
mp
Fm6 B♭7 E♭
too oo - oo oo - oo - oo?
pp
r. h.
G7 Cm Gm7 Cm
That means I of - fer my love to you to be your own.
poco espr.

F9
Db9
Eb7 Bb7
If you re - fuse me, I will be blue___ And wait-ing all a lone; But if when you
mf più espress.
pp
rall.
p espress.
a tempo.
Fm6
Bb7
3
Eb
hear___ my love call___ ring-ing clear,___ And I hear your
pp
Eb9
Ab
Eb7 Ab
an - swer-ing ech - o, so dear,___
mf molto espr.
Abm
Abm6
Eb
D7 Eb
Then I will know___ our love will come true,___ You'll be-long to
p
mf rit. e molto espr.
p a tempo.
Fm6
Bb7
Bb7+5
Eb
me,___ I'll be - long to you!
cresc.
rit.
mf
pp
Ped.
*

ISN'T IT ROMANTIC?

(From The Paramount Picture "LOVE ME TONIGHT")

Eb/G C7 Fm7 Bb7
kiss just the thing I miss on a night like
mance! I don't give a stitch if I don't get
Eb Ab Abm Eb/G Gbdim7
this. If dreams are made of i - mag - i - na - tion, I'm not a -
rich. A cus - tom tai - lor who has no cus - tom, is like a
Fm7 Bb7#5 Ebmaj7
fraid of my own cre - a - tion. With all my
sail - or, no one will trust 'em. But there is
Ab Bb7 Eb/G Adim
heart, my heart is here for you to take. Why should I
mag - ic in the mu - sic of my shears; I shed no

Bb7
Eb6
F7
Bb7
Steadily, not too fast
Eb
3 fr
quake? I'm not a - wake. Is - n't it ro - man - tic?
tears. Lend me your ears! Is - n't it ro - man - tic?
Bb7
Eb
Bb7#5
Eb
Bb7
Mu - sic in the night, a dream that can be heard. Is - n't it ro -
Soon I will have found some girl that I a - dore. Is - n't it ro -
Eb
Bb7
Eb
man - tic? Mov - ing shad - ows write the old - est mag - ic
man - tic? While I sit a - round, my love can scrub the
C7#5
C7
Fm
C7
Fm
Bb7
G7
word. I hear the breez - es play - ing
floor. She'll kiss me ev - 'ry hour,

Cm
G7#5
Cm
Eb7/Bb
Ab
C7/G
in the trees a - bove. While
or she'll get the sack. And
Fm
Bb7
Bdim7
Cm
F9
Bbdim7
Bb7
all the world is say - ing you were meant for love. Is - n't it ro -
when I take a show - er she can scrub my back. Is - n't it ro -
Eb
Bb7
Eb
Bb7#5
man - tic? Mere - ly to be young on such a night as
man - tic? On a moon-light night she'll cook me on - ion
Eb
Bb7
Eb
Bb7
this? Is - n't it ro - man - tic? Ev - 'ry note that's sung is
soup. Kid - dies are ro - man - tic, and if we don't fight, we

Eb C7#5 C7 Fm C7 Fm
like a lov - er's kiss. Sweet
soon will have a troupe! We'll
Bb7 G7 Cm Cm/Bb Cm/A Abm6
sym-bols in the moon-light, do you mean that I will fall in
help the pop-u-la-tion, it's a du-ty that we owe to
Eb/G Edim7 Bb7 Eb Gbdim7
love per - chance? Is-n't it ro-mance?
dear old France. Is-n't it ro -
Bb7 Eb Abm6 Eb6
Is-n't it ro- mance?

ISN'T THIS A LOVELY DAY
(TO BE CAUGHT IN THE RAIN?)
(From The RKO Radio Motion Picture "TOP HAT")

Words and Music by
IRVING BERLIN

G6
G♯dim7
turn in the weath - er will keep us to - geth - er,
D7/A
D9
G
Bm
so I can hon - est - ly say that as far as I'm con -
F♯7
Bm
E7
Am
D7
cerned, it's a love - ly day and ev - 'ry - thing's O.
G
Dm7
G6
Dm/G
G7
C
K. Is - n't this a love - ly day
p - f

D7
G
G/F
to be caught in the rain?
C
Cm6
D7
You were go - ing on your way,
now you've got to re - main.
G6
G/B
Just as you
B♭dim7
D7/A
G♯dim7
D9/A
D7
were go - ing leav - ing me all at sea,

G6
Gb+
Bb/F
3
the clouds broke. They broke and oh, what a break for
A7
D7
C
Cm6
D7
me. I can see the sun up high, tho' we're caught in the storm.
G
G/F
C
Cm6
I can see where you and I
D7
G6
G
C/G
could be co - zy and warm. Let the

G7
Fmaj7/G
G7
F/G
G
G9
C/E
Cm6/E♭
rain pit - ter pat - ter but it real - ly does - n't mat - ter if the
G/D
A9
C
Cm6
skies are gray.
Long as I can be with you,
D7
1 G
B♭dim7
Am7
D7
it's a love - ly day.
2 G
C/G
G
day.

IT'S IMPOSSIBLE

(SOMOS NOVIOS)

English Lyric by SID WAYNE
Spanish Words and Music by ARMANDO MANZANERO

Dm7
G7
Bm7♭5
ba - by not to cry, it's just im - pos - si - ble.
na - mos lo más gran - de de es - te mun - do.
E7
Am7
Cm
Can I hold you closer to me, and not
Nos a - ma - mos nos be - sa - mos co - mo
G
E7♭9
Am
feel you go - ing through me? Split the sec - ond that I
no - vios nos de - sea - mos y has - ta a ve - ces sin mo -
A7
D7
nev - er think of you? Oh, how im - pos - si - ble.
ti - vo sin ra - zón nos e - no - ja - mos.

Am7 D7 G G6 Gmaj7 G6
Can the o - cean _ keep from rush-ing to the shore? It's just im -
So - mos no - vios _ man - te - ne - mos un ca - ri - ño lim - pio y
F♯m7♭5 B7 Em
pos - si - ble. If I had you, _ could I
pu - ro. Co - mo to - dos _ pro - cu -
Dm7 G7 Bm7♭5 E7
ev - er want for more? It's just im - pos - si - ble. And to -
ra - mos el mo - men - to más os - cu - ro pa - ra ha-
Am7 Cm
mor - row, _ should you ask me for the world, some - how I'd
blar - nos _ pa - ra dar - nos el más dul - ce de los

G
E7♭9
get it. I would sell my ver - y soul and not re -
be - sos re - cor - dar de que co - lor son los ce -
Am
D7
1 G
gret it, for to live with-out your love is just im - pos - si - ble.
re - zos Sin ha - cer más co - men - ta - rios so - mos no - vios.
C♯m7♭5
D7
no chord
2 G
Em7
It's im - pos - si - ble. Im - pos - si - ble.
So - mos no - vios somos no - vios
Am7
D7
G
Cm6
G
Mm, im - pos - si - ble.
siem - pre no - vios.
rall.

IT'S EASY TO REMEMBER

(From The Paramount Picture "MISSISSIPPI")

Eb
Eb+
Abm
Ab
Eb
Fm7
Adim
Eb
Bb9
met. It's eas - y to re - mem - ber but so hard to for -
Eb
Fm7
Bb7
Eb
Fm7
Bb7
get. I hear you whis - per, "I'll al - ways love you." I know it's o - ver and
Eb
Eb+
Abm
Ab
Eb
Fm7
Adim
Eb
Bb9
yet, it's eas - y to re - mem - ber but so hard to for -
Eb
Eb7sus
Eb7
Abmaj7
Ab6
Bbm7
Eb7
get. So I must dream to have your hand ca - ress me, fin - gers press me

Abmaj7
Ab6
Abm7
Db7
Gbmaj7
Gb6
Bb
Cm
F7
tight. I'd rath-er dream than have that lone-ly feel-ing steal-ing through the
Bb
Bb7
Fm7
Bb7
Eb
night. Each lit-tle mo-ment is clear be-fore me, and though it
Fm7
Bb7
Eb
Eb+
Abm
Ab
Eb
Db9
brings me re-gret, it's eas-y to re-mem-ber and
Adim
Eb
Bb9
Eb
so hard to for-get. Your sweet ex-
Adim
Eb
Bb9
Eb
Ab
Eb
so hard to for-get.
mp
rall.

JUNE IN JANUARY

(From The Paramount Picture "HERE IS MY HEART")

Words and Music by LEO ROBIN
and RALPH RAINGER

C7
Fm
just white blos - soms that fall from a - bove,
Bb7
Fm7
Bb7
Eb
and here is the rea - son my dear, your mag - i - cal charms.
G7#5
G7
Cm
Cdim7
The night is cold,
Cm
Dm7b5/C
Cm
the trees are bare, but I can

Cm7
F9
F7
B♭7
B♭7♯5(♭9)
feel the scent of ros - es in the air. It's
E♭
C7
Fm
June in Jan - u - a - ry be - cause I'm in
B♭7
Fm7
Fm7/B♭
B♭7
love, but on - ly be - cause I'm in love with
1
E♭
G♭
B♭7sus
B♭7
B♭7♯5(♭9)
you. It's
2
E♭
A♭6
E♭6
you.

JUST AS MUCH AS EVER

Words and Music by CHARLES SINGLETON
and LARRY COLEMAN

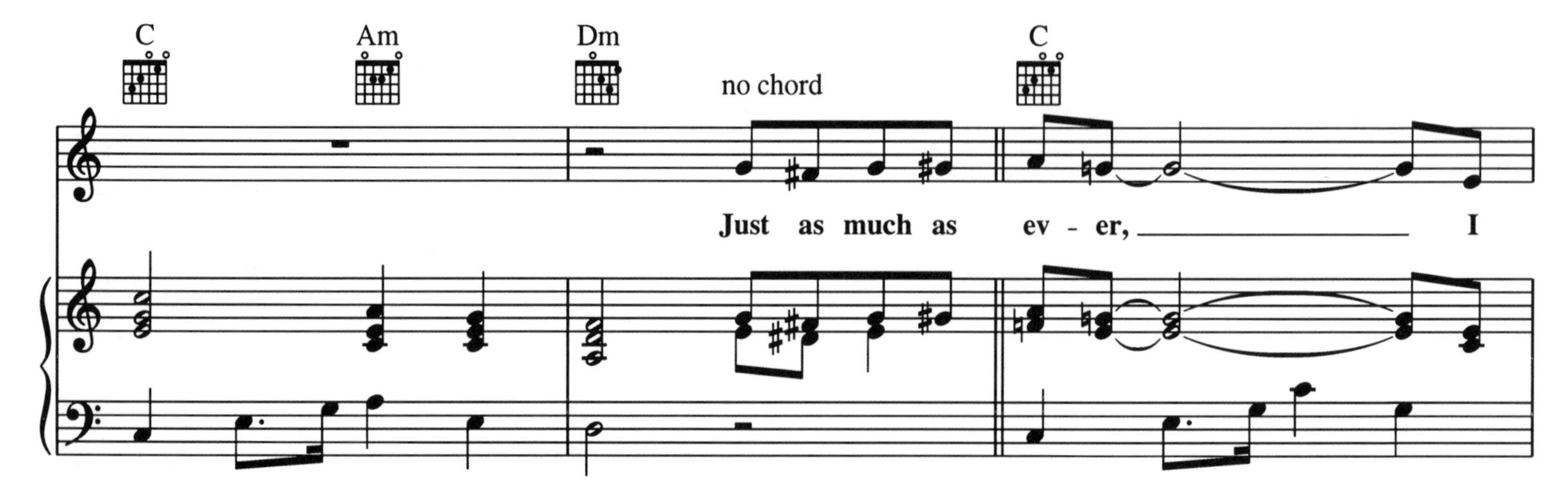

F
dear.
E - ven though we two are part - ed, my

C
Am
3
3
feel - ings for you nev - er drop for lov - ing you is some - thing I've

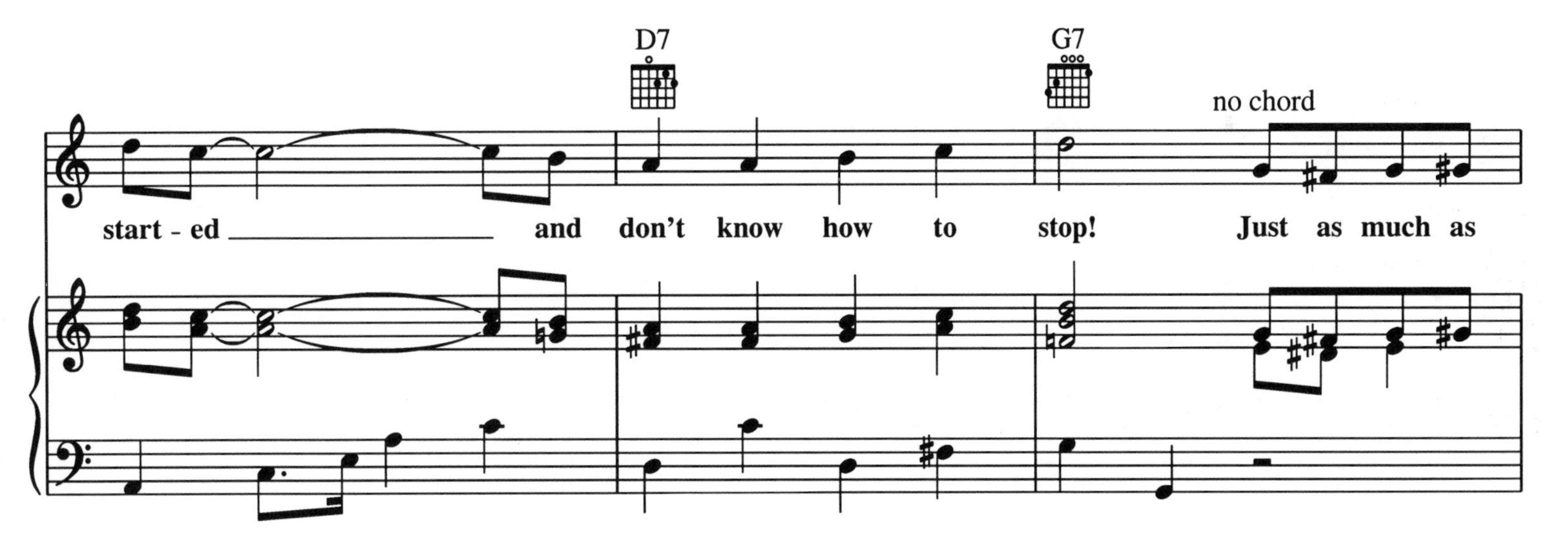
D7
G7
no chord
start - ed and don't know how to stop! Just as much as

C
G7
ev - er, I'm hop - ing that you'll be mine a -

E7
gain, dar-ling,'cause I'll nev-er be sat-is-fied till

A7
F
then for I am still the

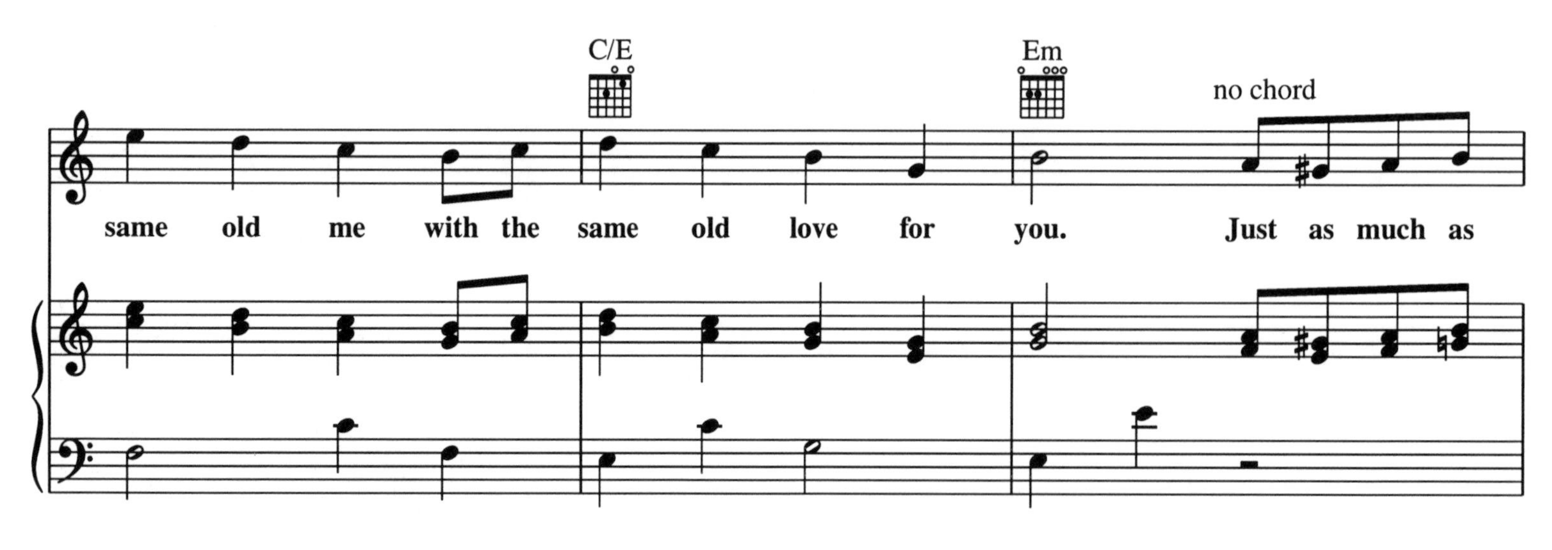
C/E
Em
no chord
same old me with the same old love for you. Just as much as

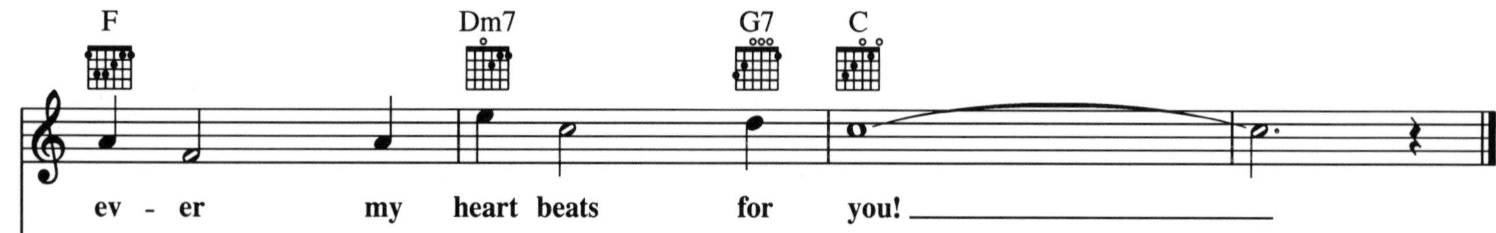
F
Dm7
G7
C
ev-er my heart beats for you!

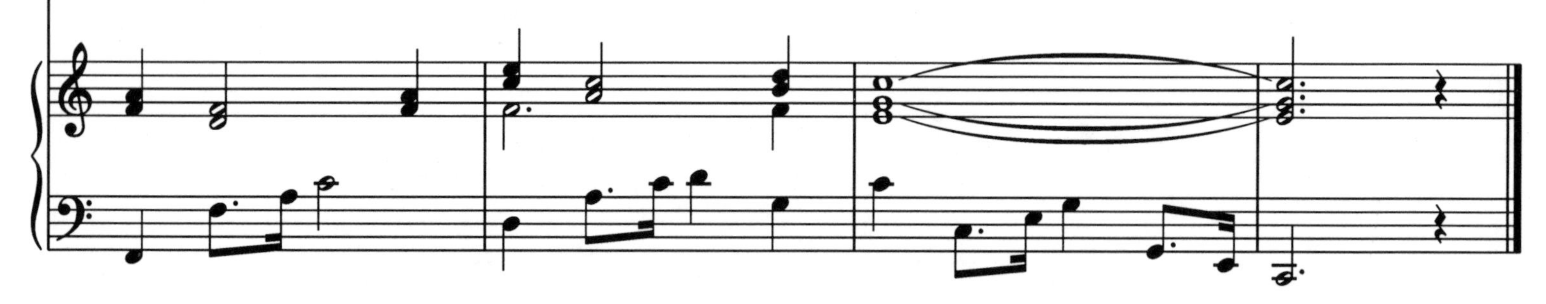

LOVER
(From The Paramount Picture "LOVE ME TONIGHT")

Words by LORENZ HART
Music by RICHARD RODGERS

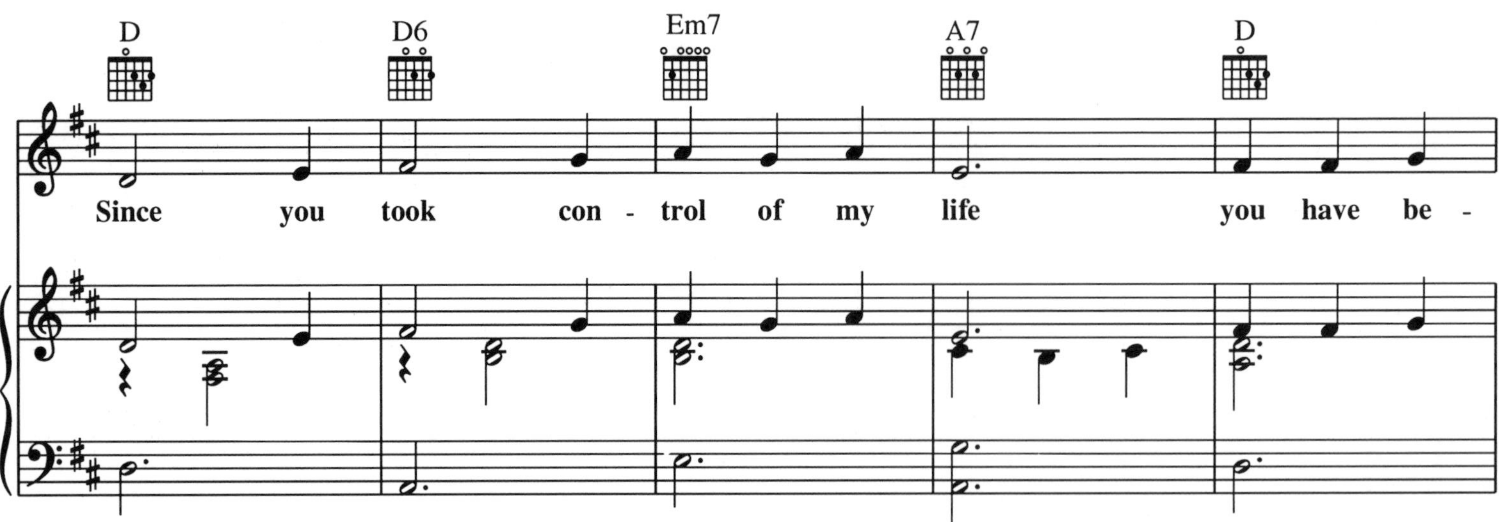
D
D6
Em7
A7
D
Since you took con - trol of my life you have be -

C#7
F#m
Bm
Em7
come the whole of my life. When you are a - way it's

A7
F#m
D6
E7
A7
aw - ful and when you are with me it's worse.

D
G#m7
4fr
C#7
Gm7
3fr
Lov - er, when I'm near you and I hear you

C7 F♯m7 B7 Fm7 B♭7
speak my name soft - ly in my
Em7 A7 D D7 G
ear you breathe a flame.
A7 D G♯m7 C♯7
Lov - er, when we're danc - ing, keep on
Lov - er, it's im - mor - al, but why
Gm7 C7 F♯m7 B7 Fm7
glanc - ing in my eyes till love's
quar - rel with our bliss when two

B♭7
Em7
A7
D
own en - tranc - ing music dies.
lips of cor - al want to kiss?
F♯
G♯m7
All of my fu - ture is in you.
I say "The Dev - il is in you,"
C♯7
F♯
G♯m7
C♯7
Your ev - 'ry plan I de - sign.
and to re - sist you I try;
A
Bm7
E7
Em7/A
Prom - ise you'll al - ways con - tin - ue to be mine.
but if you did - n't con - tin - ue I would die!
4fr
2fr

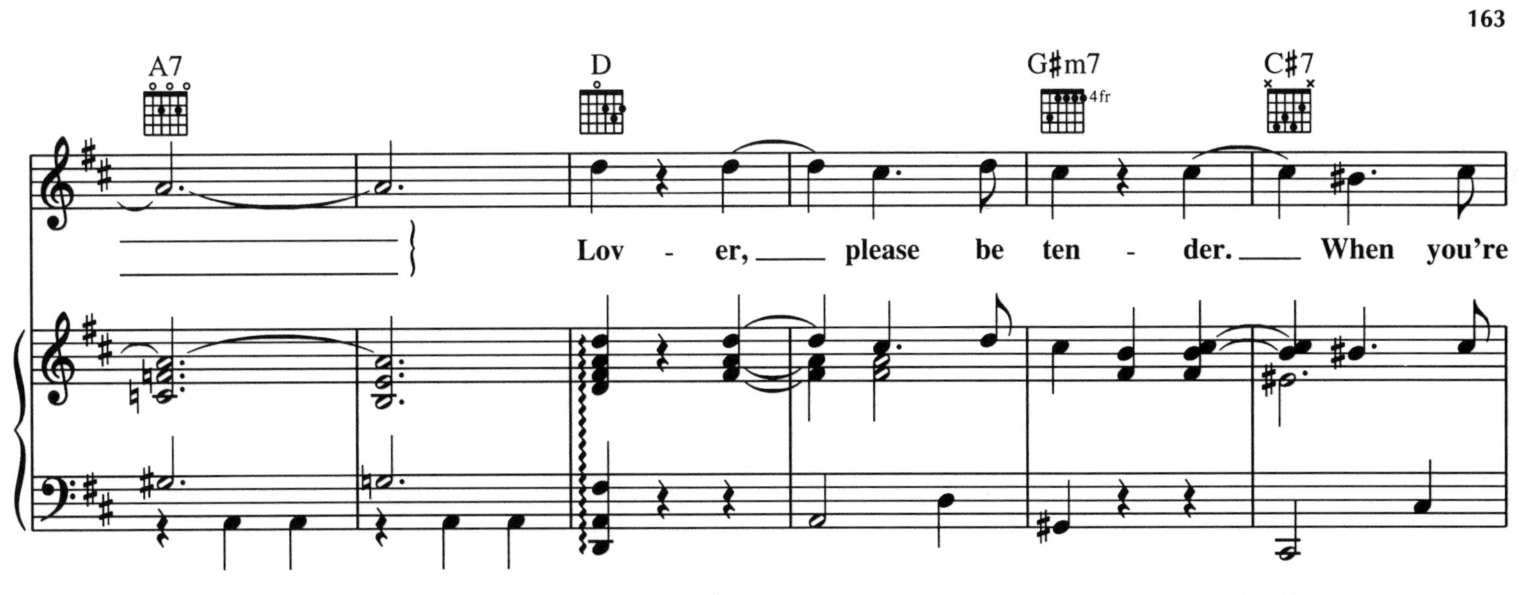
A7
D
G♯m7
4fr
C♯7
Lov - er, please be ten - der. When you're

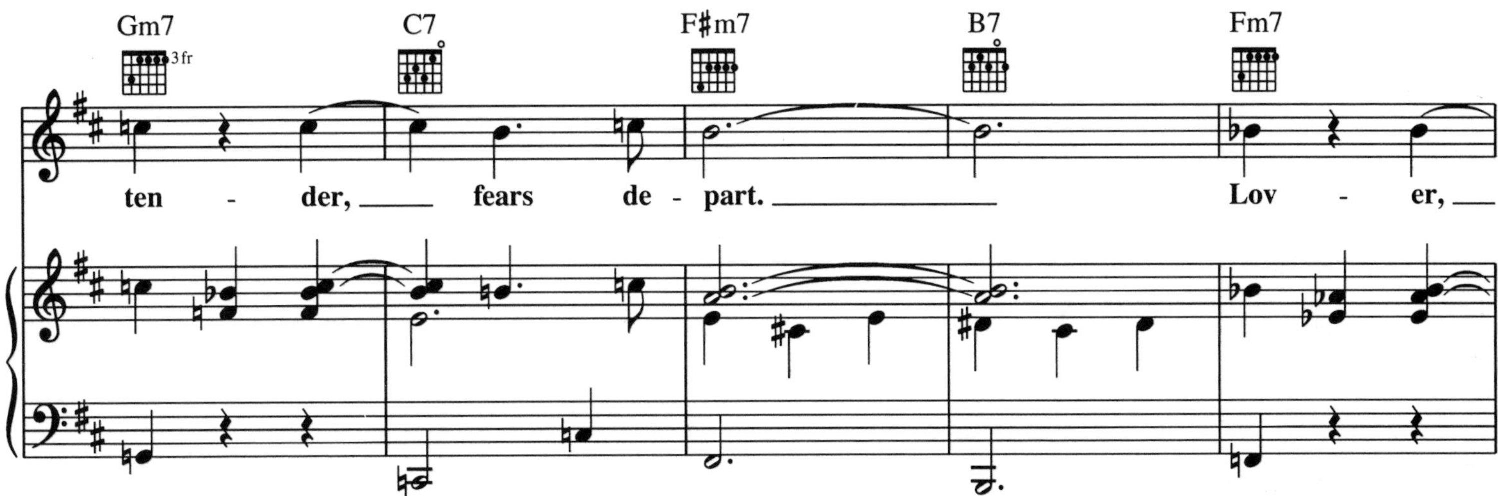
Gm7
3fr
C7
F♯m7
B7
Fm7
ten - der, fears de - part. Lov - er,

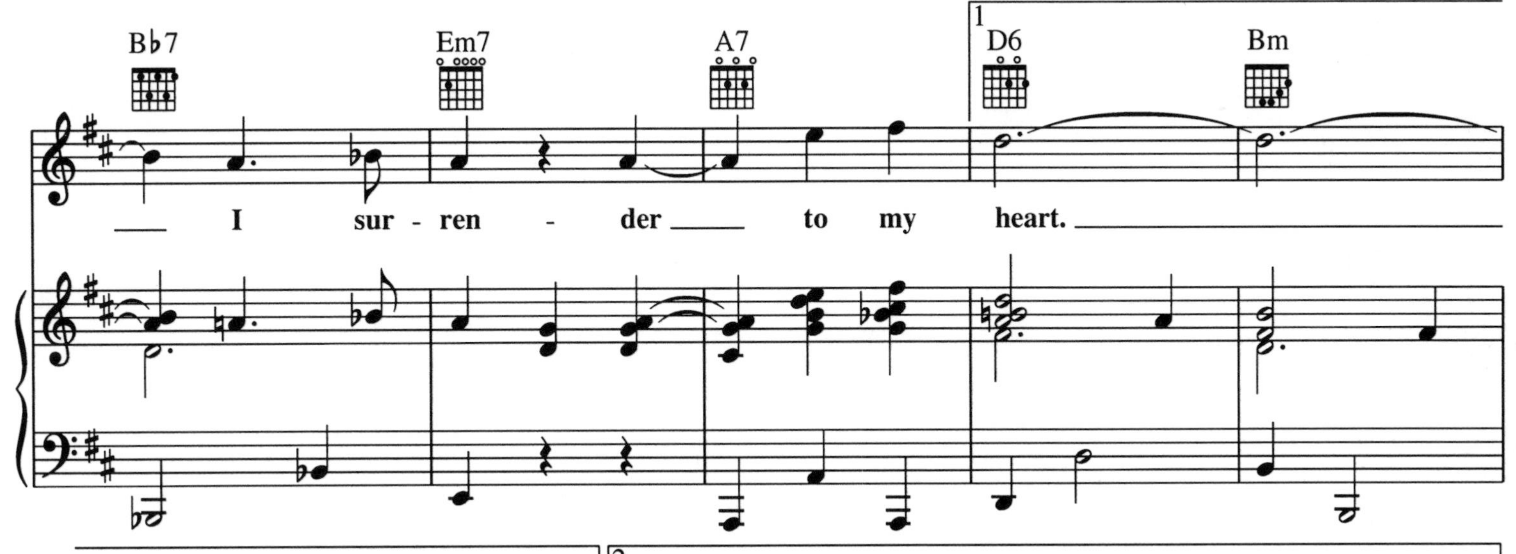
B♭7
Em7
A7
1
D6
Bm
I sur - ren - der to my heart.

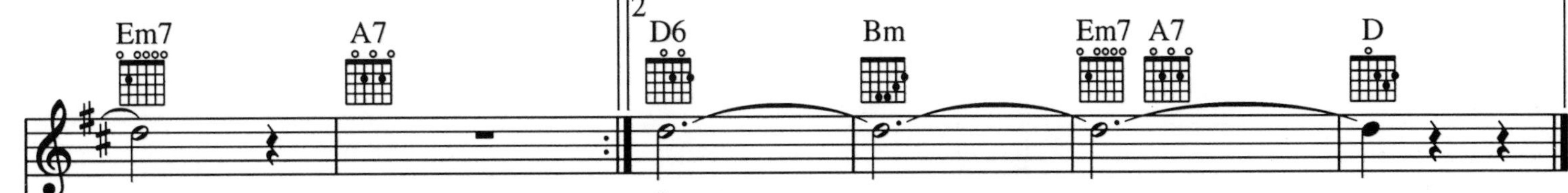
Em7
A7
2
D6
Bm
Em7
A7
D
heart.

8va basso

LET THERE BE LOVE

Lyric by IAN GRANT
Music by LIONEL RAND

Moderately

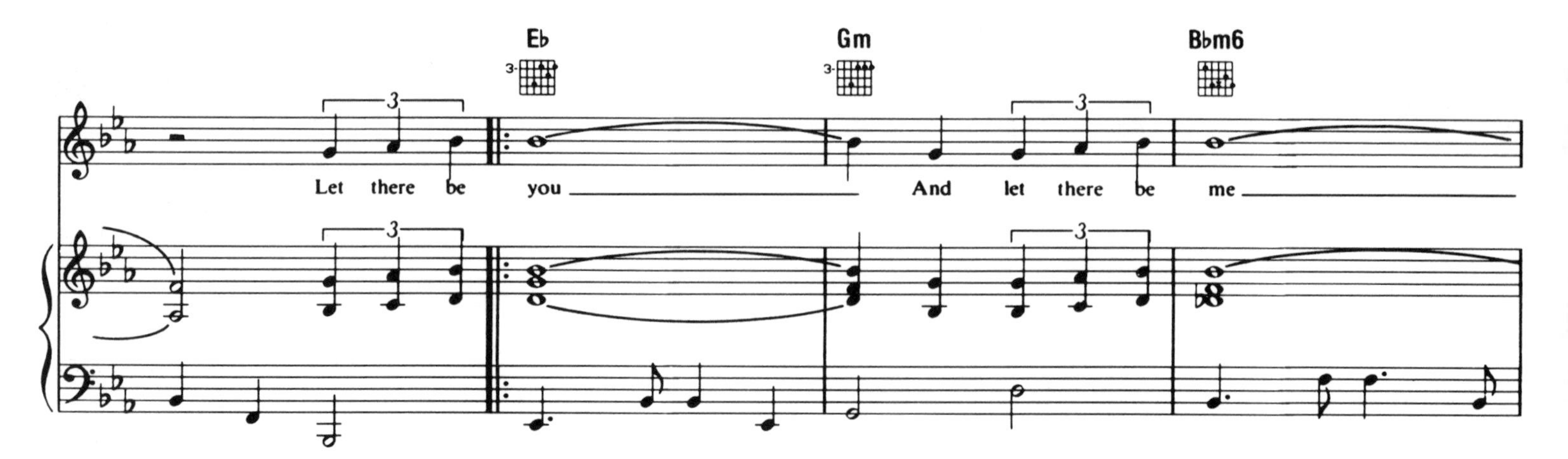

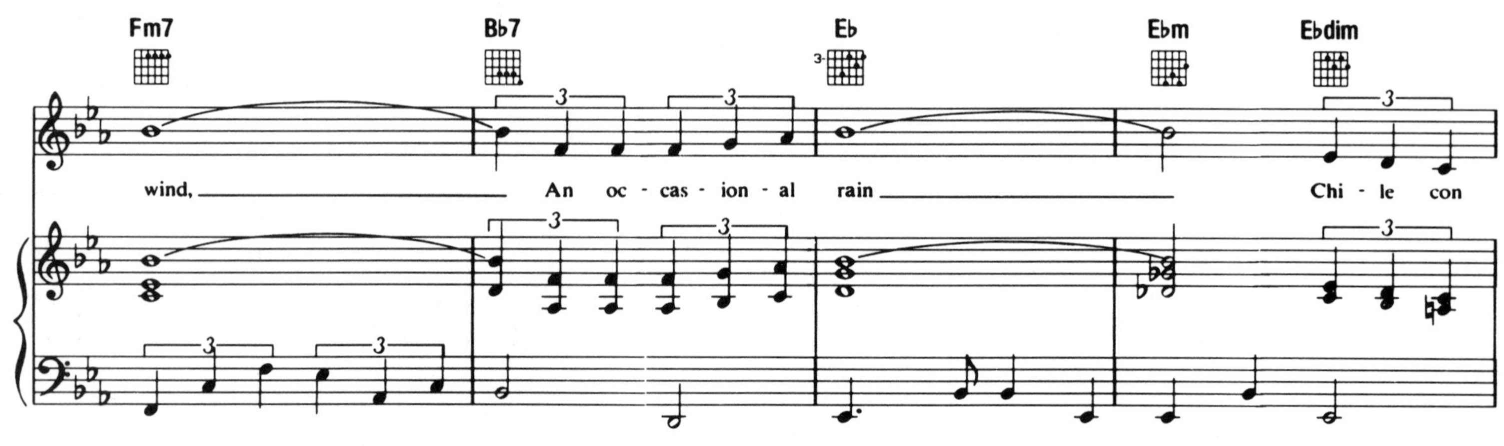

Fm7
Bb7
Eb
carne And sparkling champagne
Let there be birds
Gm
Bbm6
C7
Abm6
To sing in the trees
Someone to bless me
Bb7
Eb
Bb7
Eb
Whenever I sneeze
Let there be cuckoos,
Gm7
Bbm6
C9
C7
Fm7
A lark and a dove
But first of all, please
Bb7
1 Eb
Ebm
Fm7
Bb7
2 Eb
Abm6
Eb6
Let There Be Love
Let there be Love.

LET'S FACE THE MUSIC AND DANCE

(From The Motion Picture "FOLLOW THE FLEET")

Words and Music by
IRVING BERLIN

Fm6
C
A♭9/E♭
Dm7♭5
G+
Cm
mu - sic and dance.
Be - fore the
A♭/C
Cm
Cm6
Cm7
G7/D
G7
fid - dlers have fled,
be - fore they
A♭7
D7/A
D7
Dm7
Dm7/G
G7
F
ask us to pay the bill,
and while we still
F/G
G7
C/G
C
G6
C9
F
have the chance,
let's face the

Fm6
C/E
Cdim/E♭
Dm7
C
A♭
mu - sic and dance.
Soon
E♭7
A♭
E♭7
we'll be with - out the moon,
hum - ming a
A♭
G7
F/A
B♭m
G7/B
diff - 'rent tune, and then
Cm
A♭/C
Cm
Cm6
Cm♯7
Cm7
there may be tear - drops to shed.

Cm
Ab/C
Cm
Dm7b5
G7
Csus
C
So while there's moon-light and mu-sic and love and ro-
C9
F
Fm6
C/E
D7
mance, let's face the mu-sic and dance,
D7/A
Ab7b5
C/G
Am7/G
Dm7
Dm7/G
C6
dance. Let's face the mu-sic and dance.
1
Ebm6
Dm7b5
G7#5
2
G7#5b9
C6

L-O-V-E

Words and Music by BERT KAEMPFERT
and MILT GABLER

D7
G
all that I can give to you, Love is more than just a game for
G7
C
C#dim
two, Two in love can make it, Take my heart and please don't break it,
mf
G
D7
1 G
B♭dim D7
2 G
Am7
D7
Love was made for me and you.
you. (That's al - most
G
Am7
D7
G
C
G
true) For me and you.

LOVE IS JUST AROUND THE CORNER

(From The Paramount Picture "HERE IS MY HEART")

Words and Music by LEO ROBIN
and LEWIS E. GENSLER

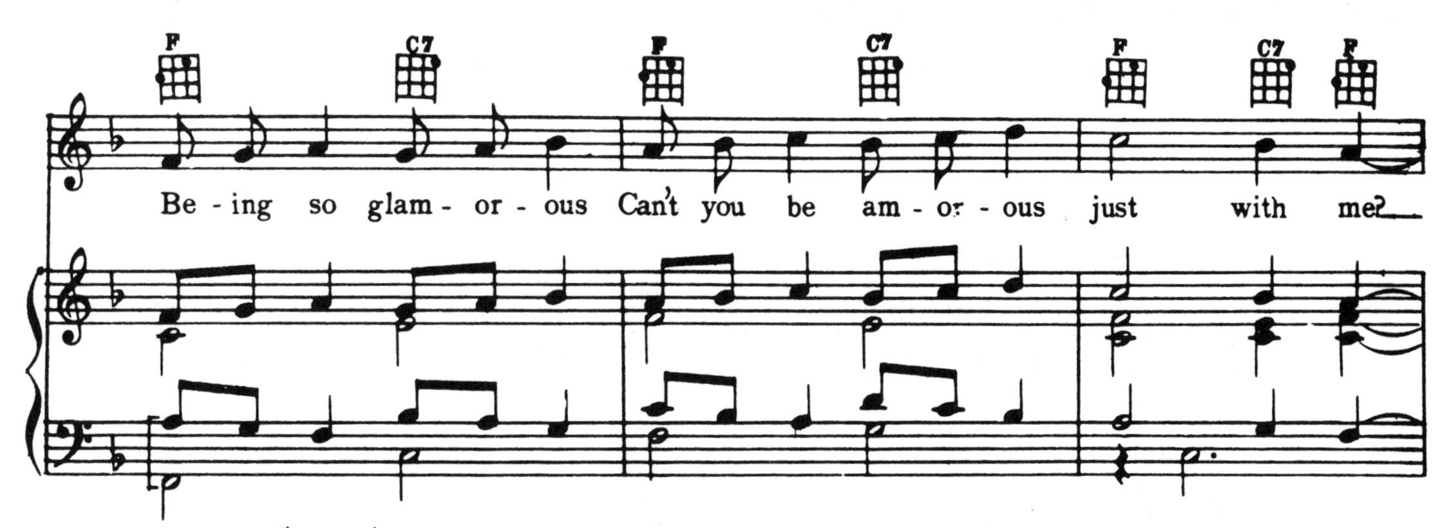
F
C7
F
C7
F
C7
F
Be - ing so glam - or - ous Can't you be am - or - ous just with me?

F
F#dim.
Ab7
C
F#dim.
G9
G9-5
C7
Bb
Am
E
Make it soon, Take a look at the moon-oo - - - -

Refrain
G7
C7
F
G7
C7
F
mp-mf
Love is just a round the cor-ner, An - y co - zy lit - tle cor-ner,

G7
C7
F
Cm
D7
G9
C7
F
Love is just a-round the cor - ner when I'm a-round you.

G7
C7
F
G7
C7
I'm a sen - ti - men - tal mourn - er, And I could - n't be for -

F
G7
C7
F
Cm
D7
G9
C7
lorn - er When you keep me on a - cor - ner just wait - ing for

F
A7
Dm
A7
you Ve - nus de Mi - lo was not - ed for her

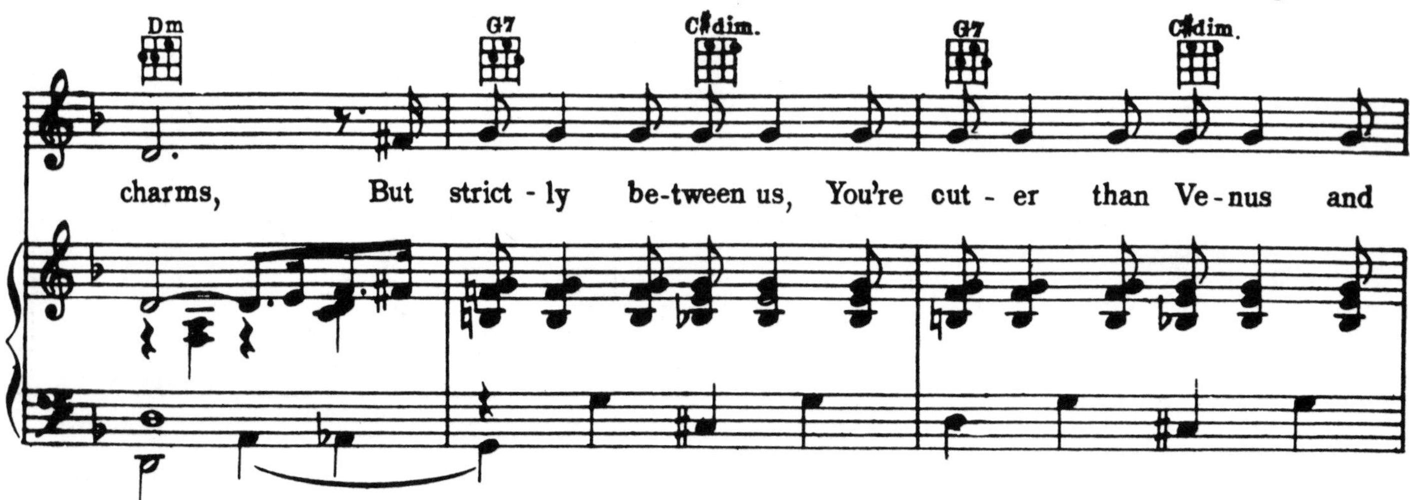
Dm
G7
C♯dim.
G7
C♯dim.
charms, But strict - ly be - tween us, You're cut - er than Ve - nus and

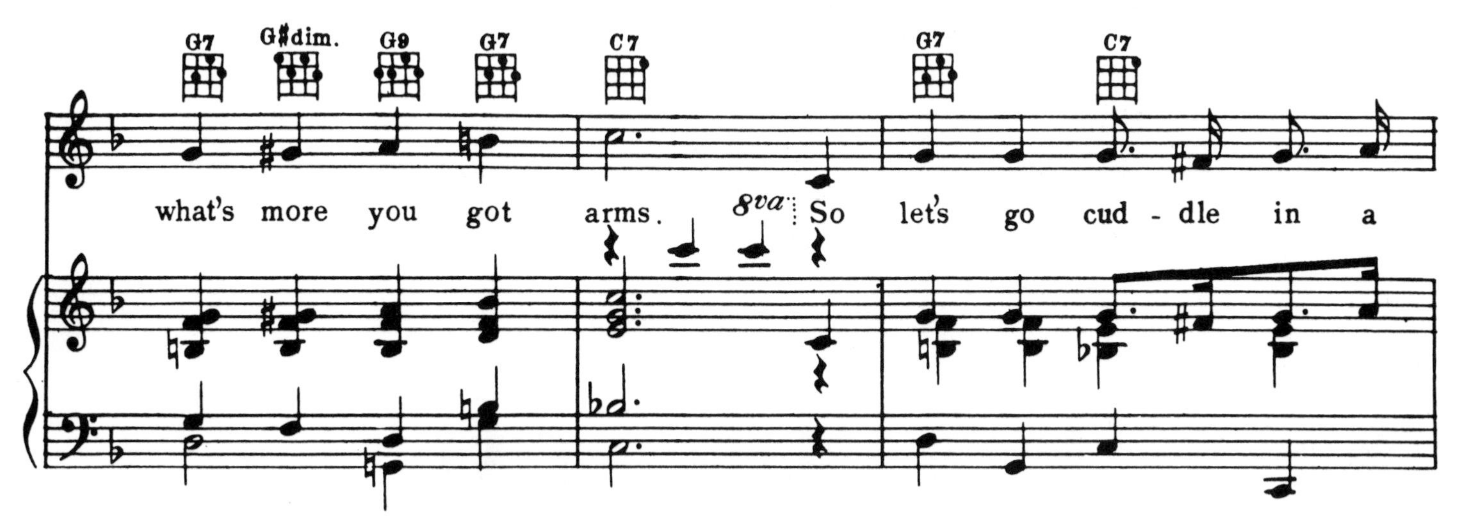

G7
G♯dim.
G9
G7
C7
G7
C7
what's more you got arms.
8va
So let's go cud - dle in a

F
G7
C7
F
cor - ner
An - y co - zy lit - tle cor - ner

G7
C7
F
Cm
D7
G9
C7
1
F
G9
C7
Love is just a-round the cor - ner and I'm a-round you

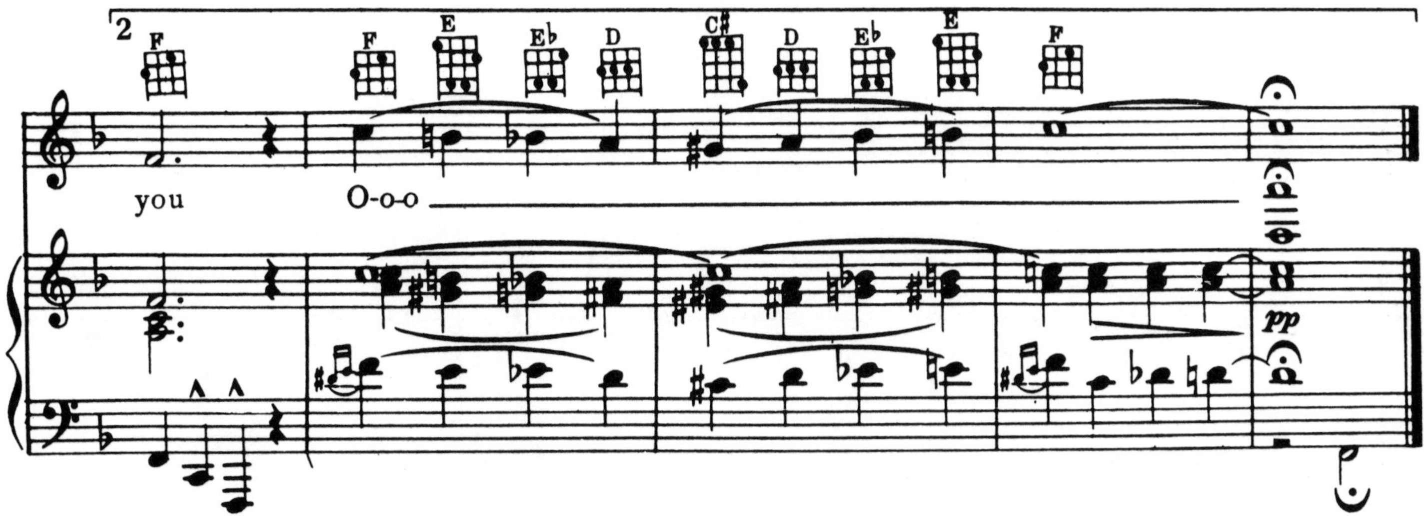

2
F
F
E
E♭
D
C♯
D
E♭
E
F
you O-o-o
pp

LOVER, COME BACK TO ME

(From "THE NEW MOON")

Lyrics by OSCAR HAMMERSTEIN II
Music by SIGMUND ROMBERG

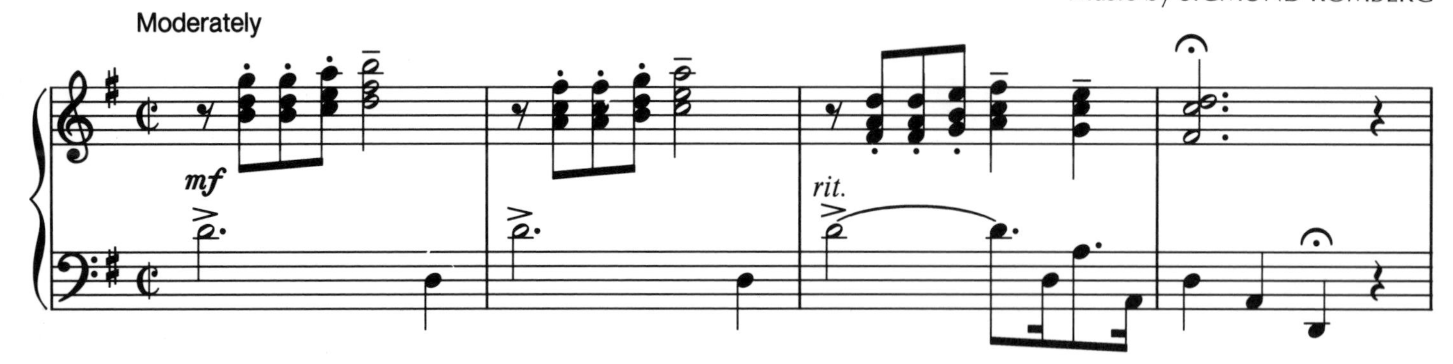

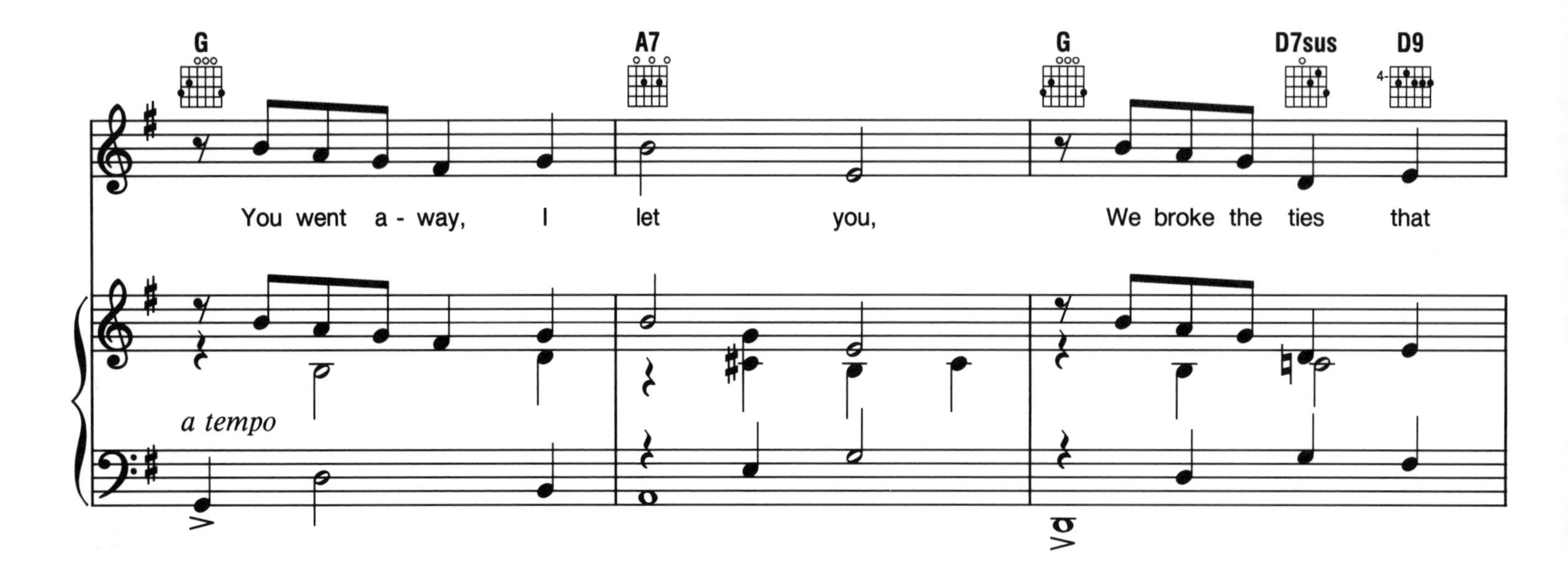

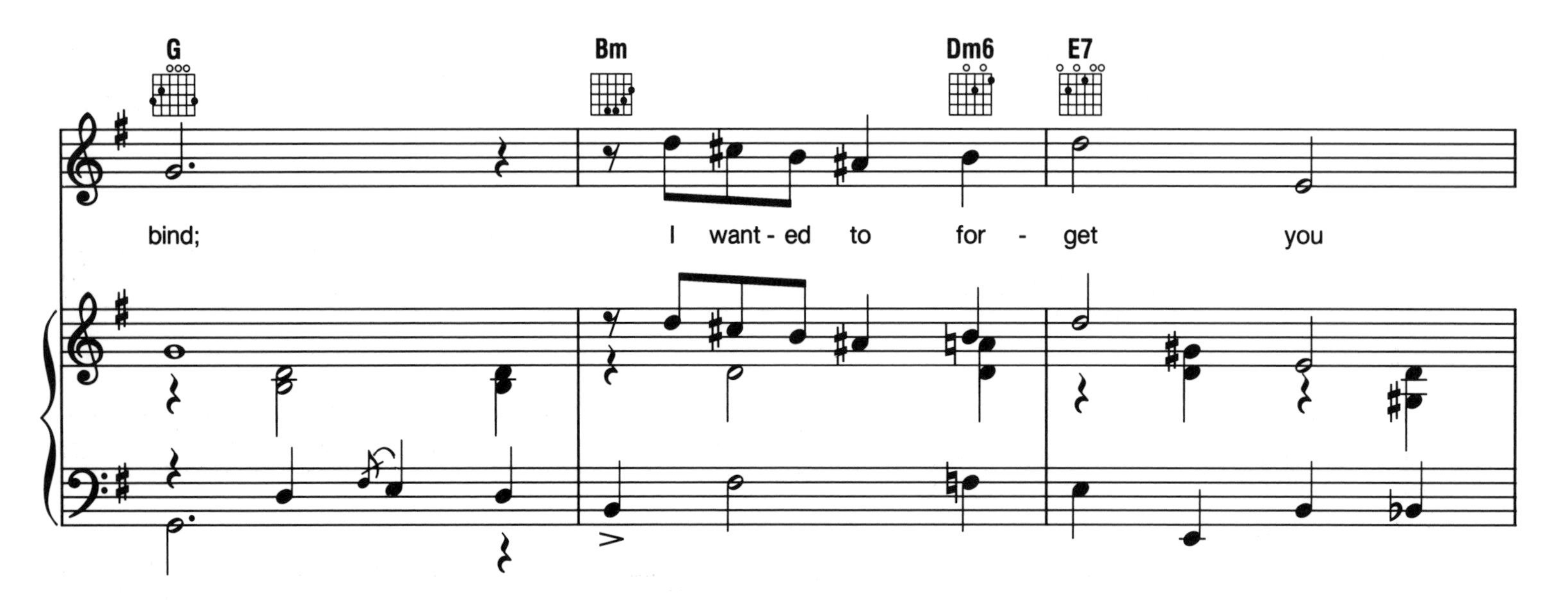

D
A7
D
And leave the past be - hind.
B♭
F7
Still, the mag - ic of the night I met you
Gm
A7
D7
Seems to stay for - ev - er in my mind.
rall.
G
B7
Em
The sky was blue, And high a - bove The moon was new
a tempo

A7
G
And so was love.
This eag - er heart of mine was
A7
D7
G
C
Cm6
G
D7
sing - ing:
"Lov - er, where can you be?"
G
B7
Em
You came at last,
Love had its day,
That day is past
A7
G
You've gone a - way.
This ach - ing heart of mine is

A7
D7
G
C
Cm6
sing - ing: "Lov - er, come back to
G
B7
Em
me!" When I re - mem - ber ev - 'ry lit - tle
Am
Em
B7
F♯sus
B7
thing you used to do, I'm so lone - ly,
poco accel.
Em
Am
Em
Ev - 'ry road I walk a - long I've walked a - long with you,
a tempo

A7
D7
G
No wonder I am lonely.
The sky is blue,
B7
Em
G♯dim7
The night is cold,
The moon is new,
But love is old,
Am
G
Am
D7
And, while I'm waiting here, This heart of mine is singing:
rit.
a tempo
G
C
Cm6
G
D7
G
"Lover come back to me!"
me!"
Ped.

(YOU'VE GOT)
THE MAGIC TOUCH

Words and Music by
BUCK RAM

Moderately

Cm Bdim7 E♭6 C7 F7

mf

E♭sus E♭ G♭dim7

You've got the mag - ic touch, it makes me

B♭7

glow so much; it casts a spell, it rings a

E♭ B♭7

bell, the mag - ic touch; Oh, when I

E♭sus
E♭
G♭dim7
B♭7
feel your charm, it's like a four - a - larm;
you make me thrill so much, you've got the mag - ic
E♭
A♭
E♭
A♭
touch. Here I go reel - ing, oh,
E♭
C7
oh, I'm feel - ing the glow, but where can I

F7
B♭9
B♭7
go from you? I did-n't
E♭sus
E♭
G♭dim7
B♭7
know too much and then I felt your touch,
and now I learn I can re-turn the mag-ic
1 E♭ E♭maj7 A♭ Fm7 B♭9 B♭7
2 E♭ A♭ E♭ Fm7 E♭maj7
touch. You've got the touch.
poco rit.

MAKE BELIEVE

(From "SHOW BOAT")

Lyrics by OSCAR HAMMERSTEIN II
Music by JEROME KERN

Cmaj7
C7
F
Fm6
C
dream a- bout don't hap- pen to be so,
That's just an
Dm
G7
C
Gdim
un- im- por- tant tech- ni- cal- i- ty.
We could
G7
G9
make be- lieve I love you,
On- ly
C
Cdim
make be- lieve that you love me.
Oth- ers
G7
Dm7
G
F
G7
find peace of mind in pre- tend- ing;
Could- n't
f
mf

C
D7
G
Gdim
you? Could- n't I? Could- n't we make be-
G7
G9
-lieve our lips are blend- ing In a
C
D7
phan- tom kiss, or two or three? Might as
F6
Cdim
C
Gdim
well make be- lieve I love you. For, To
G7
C
tell the truth, I do.

MONA LISA

(From The Paramount Picture "CAPTAIN CAREY, U.S.A.")

Words and Music by JAY LIVINGSTON
and RAY EVANS

E♭
3fr
Li - sa, Mo - na Li - sa men have named you. You're so
Fm7
B♭
Fm
like the la - dy with the mys - tic smile. Is it on - ly 'cause you're lone - ly __ they have
B♭7
E♭
3fr
blamed you for that Mo - na Li - sa strange - ness __ in your smile? Do you
smile to tempt a lov - er, __ Mo - na Li - sa, __ or is

Ab
4fr
Abm
4fr
this your way to hide a bro - ken heart?
Man - y dreams have been brought to your
Eb
3fr
Bb7
Eb
3fr
Eb7
door - step.
They just lie there,
and they die there.
Are you
Ab
4fr
Eb
3fr
warm, are you real, Mo - na Li - sa,
or just a
Bb7
1
Eb
3fr
2
Eb
3fr
cold and lone - ly, love - ly work of art?
Mo - na art?

MIMI

(From The Paramount Picture "LOVE ME TONIGHT")

Words by LORENZ HART
Music by RICHARD RODGERS

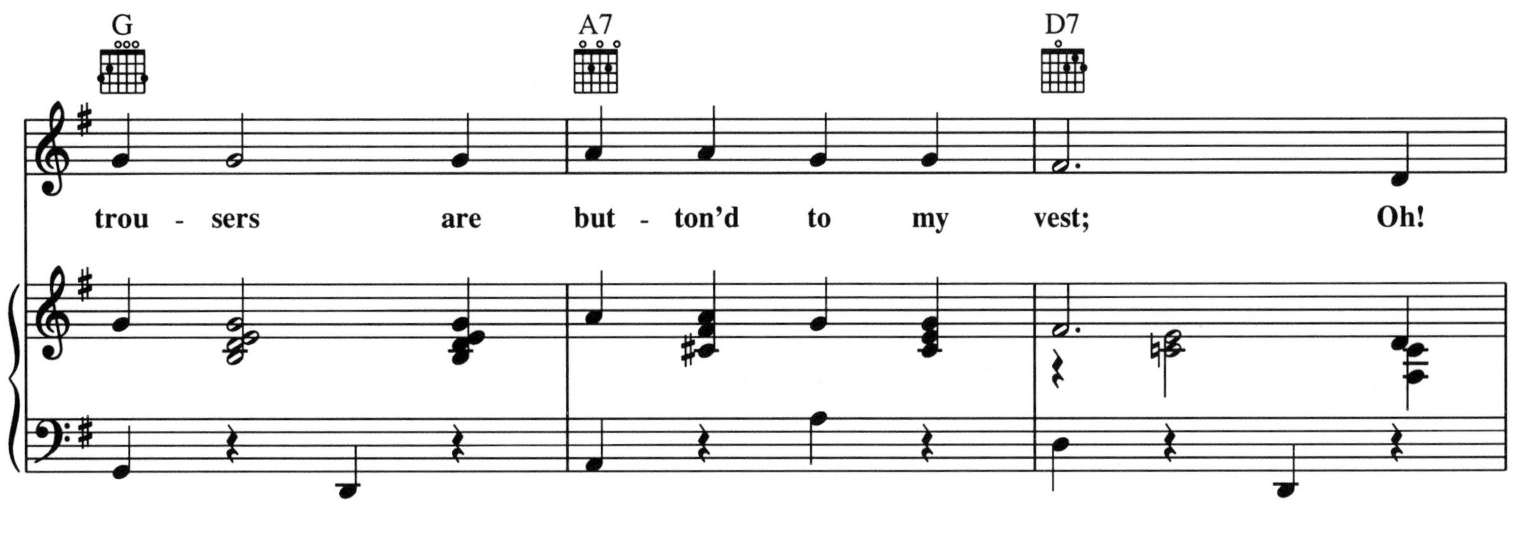
G
A7
D7
trou - sers are but - ton'd to my vest; Oh!

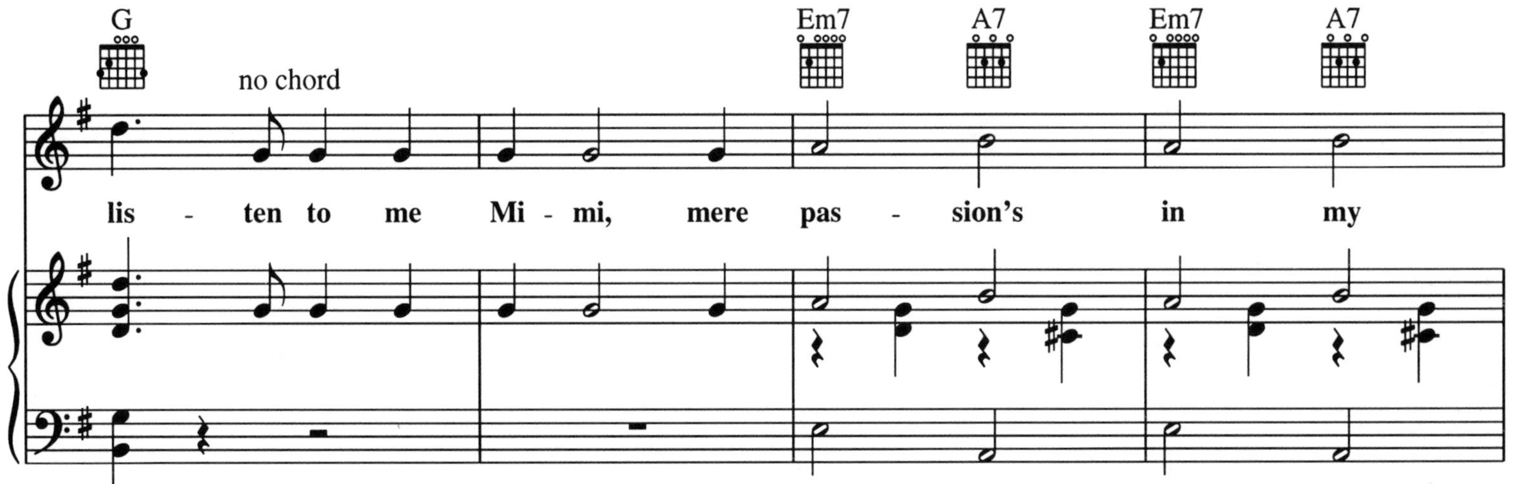
G
no chord
Em7
A7
Em7
A7
lis - ten to me Mi - mi, mere pas - sion's in my

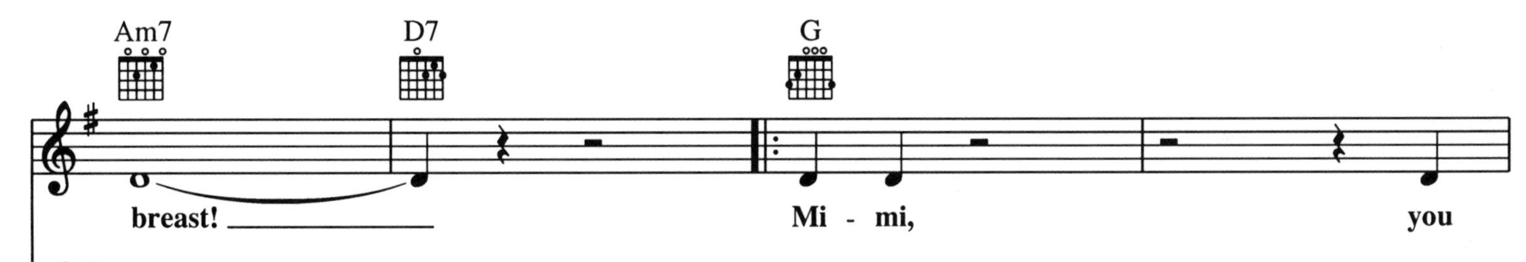
Am7
D7
G
breast!
Mi - mi, you

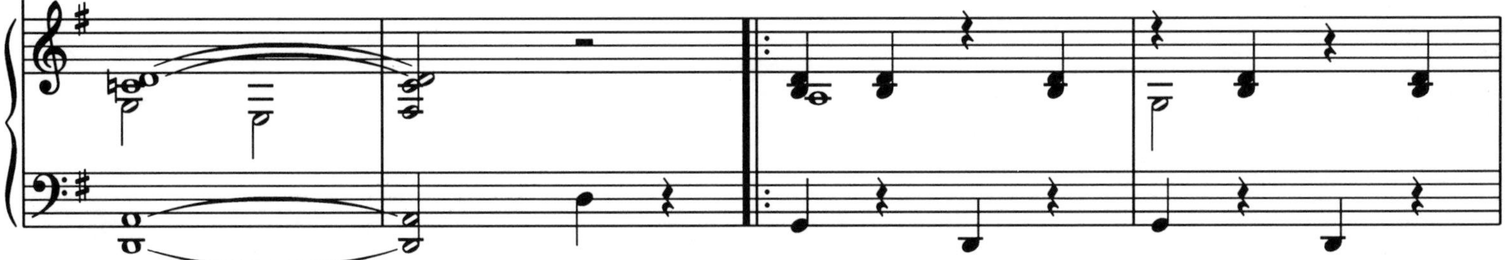

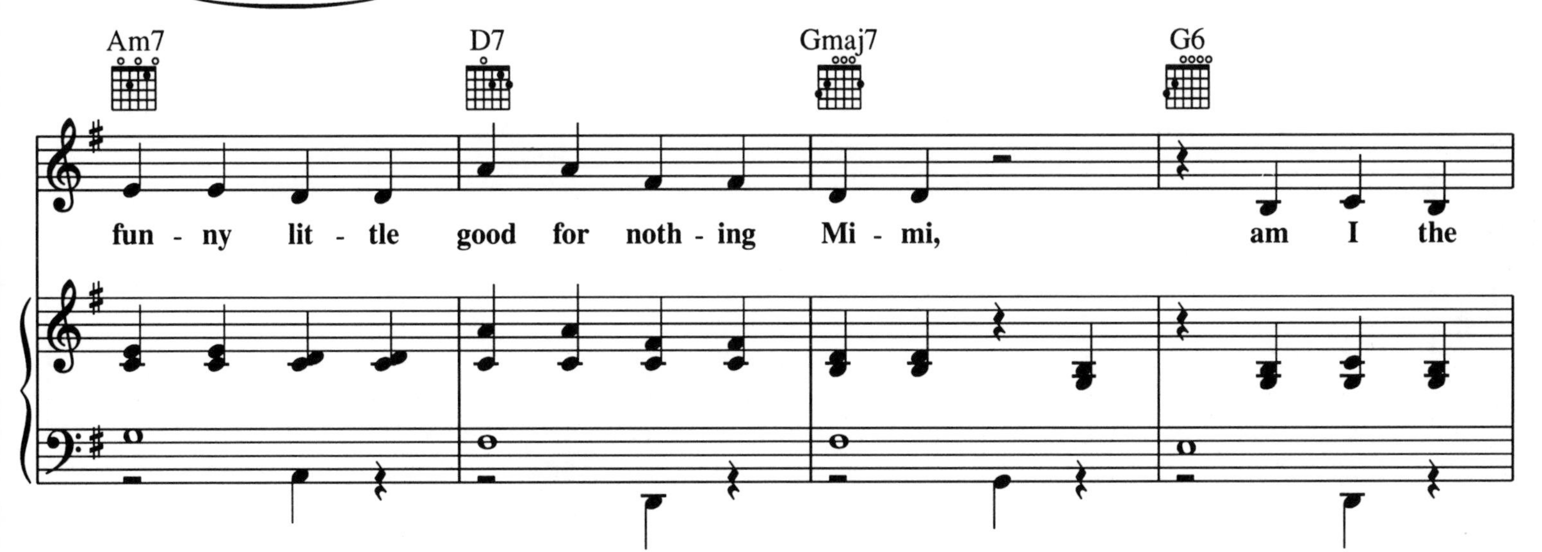
Am7
D7
Gmaj7
G6
fun - ny lit - tle good for noth - ing Mi - mi, am I the

Am7
D7
G
guy? Mi - mi, you
Am7
D7
Gmaj7
G6
sun - ny lit - tle hon - ey of a Mi - mi, I'm aim - ing
Dm7/G
G7
C
high! Mi - mi,
Cdim7
You've got me sad and dream - y,

G6/B
B♭dim7
you could free me, if you'd see me.
G
Am7
Mi - mi, you know I'd like to
D7
G
C6
G
C6
have a lit - tle son of a Mi - mi bye and
1
G
Am7
D7
bye.
2
G
Am7
G
bye.

MOON RIVER

(From The Paramount Picture "BREAKFAST AT TIFFANY'S")

Words by JOHNNY MERCER
Music by HENRY MANCINI

Cmi. D7 Gmi.
Can't be or - dered a la carte I won - der if she he will
C7 Bb Cmi.7 F7 Fmi.7 Bb+
be Al-ways a fan - ta - sy.
rall.
RAIN
Eb C9 Fmi. Db7 C7
p-mf
Will I ev - er find the girl boy in my mind The one who is My I -
p-mf a tempo
F7 Bb7 Fmi. Bb7 G7
deal. May - be she's he's a dream and yet she he might be.

C7/G F Bb9(#11) Am Am7/G
mak - er, you heart - break - er, wher - ev - er you're
F#m7b5 B7 Em7 A7 Dm7 G9 C
4fr
go - in', I'm go - in' your way. Two
Am F C/E F
drift - ers, off to see the world. There's such a lot of
C/E Bm7b5 E7 Am
world to see. We're af -

MY IDEAL

(From The Paramount Picture "PLAYBOY OF PARIS")

Music by RICHARD A. WHIT

Cmi. F7 B7 B♭7 E♭ C9
Just a-round the cor-ner wait-ing for me — Will I rec-og-nize a

Fmi. D♭7 C7 F7
light in {her / his} eyes — That no oth-er eyes re - veal. Or / Al -

Fmi. A♭mi. E♭ Cdim. E♭ Cmi. Fmi. B♭7
will I pass {him / her} by and nev-er e - ven know that {he / she} is My I -
tho' {she / he} may be late I trust in fate and so I wait for My I -

1. 2.
E♭ Cdim. Fmi. B♭7 E♭ Cmi. E♭7 Fmi. B♭7 E♭
deal. deal. My I - deal.
Slow

MOONLIGHT BECOMES YOU

(From The Paramount Picture "ROAD TO MOROCCO")

Words by JOHNNY BURKE
Music by JAMES VAN HEUSEN

Moderately

F F#dim7 Gm7 C7 Dm G7 C7sus C7#5

mf

F Dm7 Dm6 Gm7

Stand there just a mo - ment, dar - ling, let me catch my

C7 F Am Bb6 Gm Gb7

breath. I've nev - er seen a pic - ture quite so

F Bm7 E7 A F#m7

love - ly. How did you ev - er

C7/G
F
B♭9(♯11)
Am
Am7/G
mak - er, you heart - break - er, wher - ev - er you're
F♯m7♭5
4fr
B7
Em7
A7
Dm7
G9
C
go - in', I'm go - in' your way. Two
Am
F
C/E
F
drift - ers, off to see the world. There's such a lot of
C/E
Bm7♭5
E7
Am
world to see. We're af -

Am/G
F♯m7♭5
4fr
F13
C/E
ter the same rain - bow's end.
F
C/E
F
C/E
wait-in' 'round the bend, my Huck-le-ber-ry friend,
Am
Dm7
G9
1 C
Moon Riv - er and me.
2
A♭maj7
D♭maj7
C
me.
rall.

MY IDEAL

(From The Paramount Picture "PLAYBOY OF PARIS")

Words by LEO ROBIN
Music by RICHARD A. WHITING and NEWELL CHASE

Cmi.
D7
Gmi.
Can't be or-dered a la carte I won-der if she he will

C7
Bb
Cmi.7
F7
Fmi.7
Bb+
be Al-ways a fan - ta - sy.
rall.

REFRAIN
p-mf
Eb
C9
Fmi.
Db7
C7
Will I ev-er find the girl boy in my mind The one who is My I -
p-mf a tempo

F7
Bb7
Fmi.
Bb7
G7
deal. May-be she's he's a dream and yet she he might be.

Cmi. F7 B7 B♭7 E♭ C9
Just a-round the cor-ner wait-ing for me —
Will I rec-og-nize a

Fmi. D♭7 C7 F7
light in {her his} eyes — That no oth-er eyes re - veal.
Or
Al -

Fmi. A♭mi. E♭ Cdim. E♭ Cmi. Fmi. B♭7
will I pass {him her} by and nev-er e-ven know that {he she} is My I -
tho' {she he} may be late I trust in fate and so I wait for My I -

1.
2.
E♭ Cdim. Fmi. B♭7 E♭ Cmi. E♭7 Fmi. B♭7 E♭
deal. deal. My I - deal.
Slow

MOONLIGHT BECOMES YOU

(From The Paramount Picture "ROAD TO MOROCCO")

Words by JOHNNY BURKE
Music by JAMES VAN HEUSEN

Bm7
D/E
E7
A
Gm7/C
C7
learn to look so love - ly?
F
F♯dim7
Gm7
C7
F
F/A
A♭dim7
Moon - light be - comes you, it goes with your
Gm7
C7♯5
Am7
D7
Gm7
C7♭9
hair, you cer - tain - ly know the right thing to
F
Gm7
C7♭9
F
F♯dim7
Gm7
C7
wear.
Moon-light be - comes you, I'm

202
F F/A A♭dim7 Gm7 C7♯5 Am7 D7
thrilled at the sight. And I could get so ro -
Gm7 C7♭9 F6 Gm7 F6/A F+ B♭ B♭7♯5
man - tic to - night. You're all dressed up to go
E♭ F7 B♭
dream - ing, now don't tell me I'm wrong, And
Em7♭5 A7 C♯dim Dm G7
what a night to go dream - ing, mind if I tag a -

Gm7/C
C7#5
F
F#dim7
Gm7
3 fr
C7
long? If I say I love you, I
F
F/A
A♭dim7
4 fr
Gm7
3 fr
C7#5
Am7
D7
want you to know it's not just be - cause there's
Gm7
3 fr
C7
A7
D7
G7
Gm7/C
C7
1
F
moon-light, al - though moon-light be-comes you so.
Gm7/C
C7#5(♭9)
2
F
B♭m6
6 fr
F6
so.

THE MOST BEAUTIFUL GIRL IN THE WORLD

(From "JUMBO")

Words by LORENZ HART
Music by RICHARD RODGERS

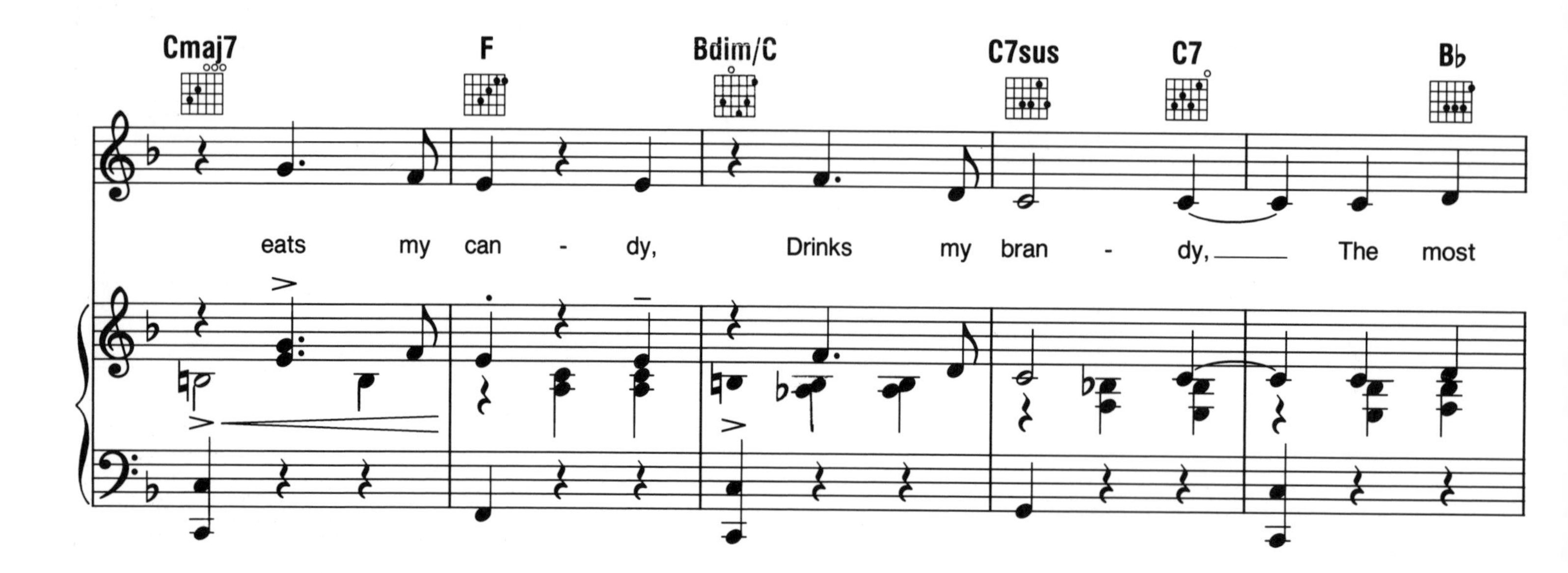

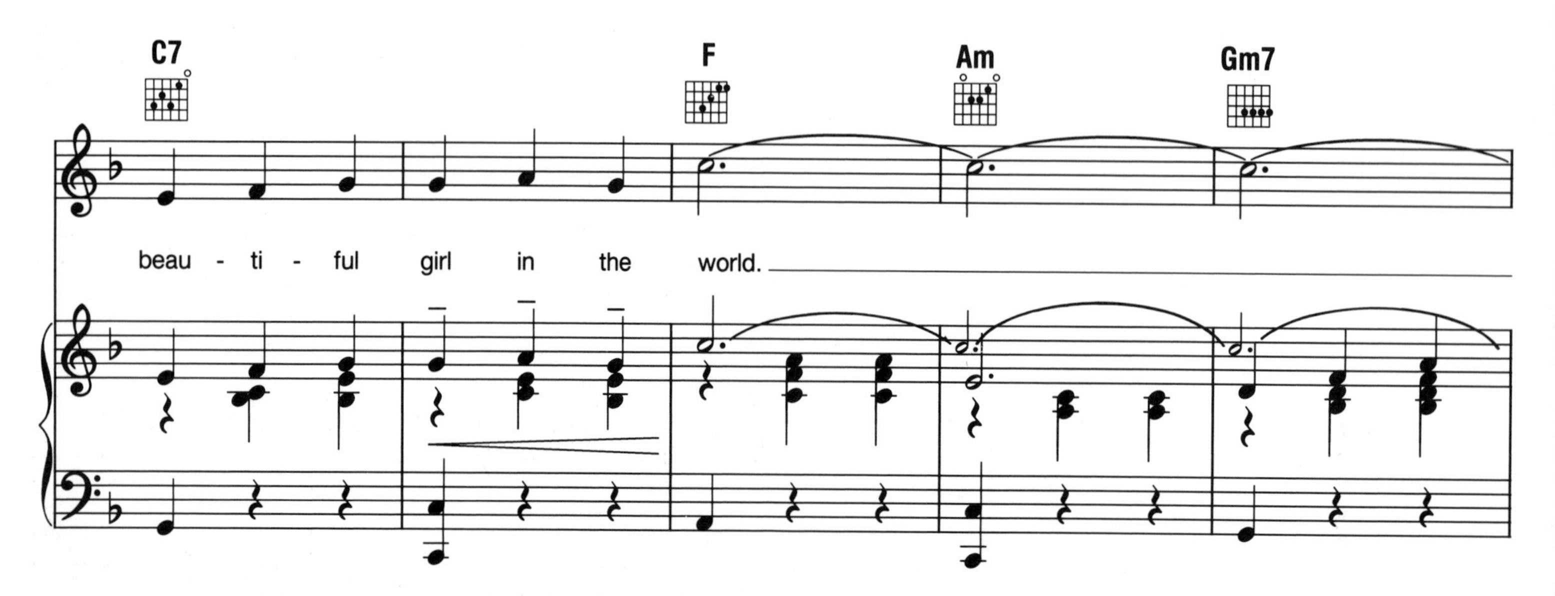

C7 F E/F Cmaj7
The most beau - ti - ful star in the world is - n't
F Cmaj7 F Bdim C7sus C7
Gar - bo, Is - n't Diet - rich But the sweet trick
B♭ C7 Cm
who can make me be - lieve it's a beau - ti - ful world
cresc.
mf
Cm6 D7 Dm G7 Gm7
So - cial not a bit,

C7
Dm
G7
Gm7
C7
Nat - 'ral kind of wit,
Am7
D7
G7sus
G7
Gm7
She'd shine an - y - where, And she has - n't got
C7
Gm
C7
F
plat - i - num hair, The most beau - ti - ful house in the

E/F
Cmaj7
F
Cmaj7
world Has a mort - gage what do

p

F
C7sus
C7
B♭
I care, it's good - bye care When my
C7
Cm
slip - pers are next to the ones that be - long
Cm6
D7
Dm7
G7
Gm7
To the one and on - ly beau - ti - ful
mf
B♭7
F
Gm7
F
girl in the world!

MY HEART STOOD STILL

(From "A CONNECTICUT YANKEE")

Words by LORENZ HART
Music by RICHARD RODGERS

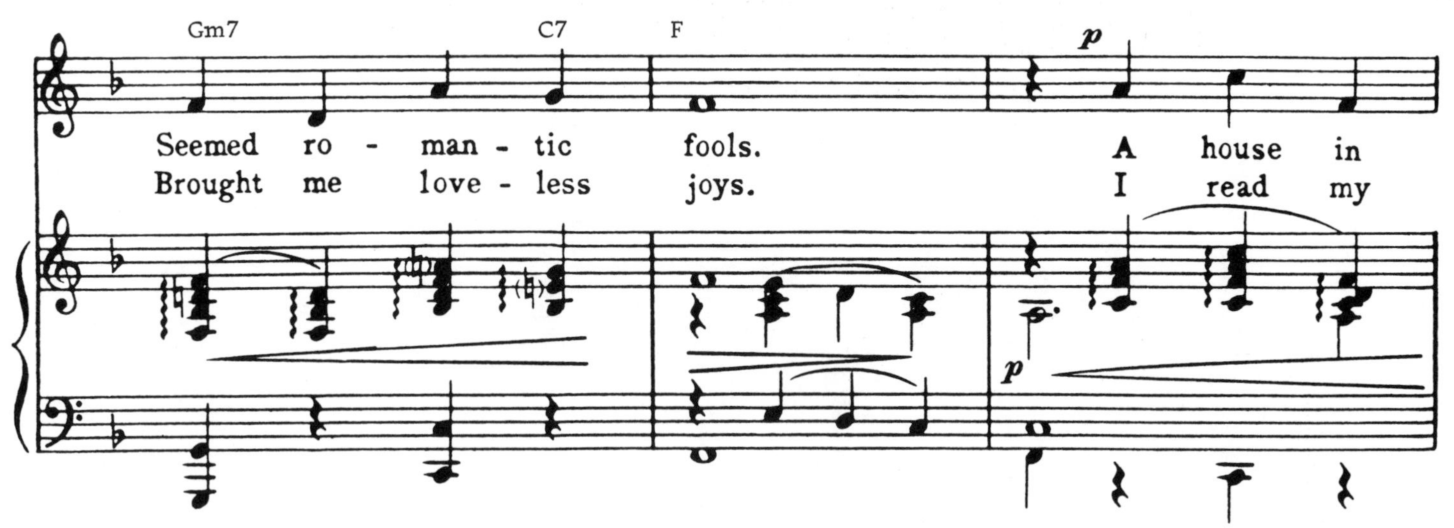
Gm7
C7
F
p
Seemed ro - man - tic fools. A house in
Brought me love - less joys. I read my
p

A
Dmaj7
E7
C
Ice - land Was my heart's do - main. I
Pla - to, Love, I thought a sin; But

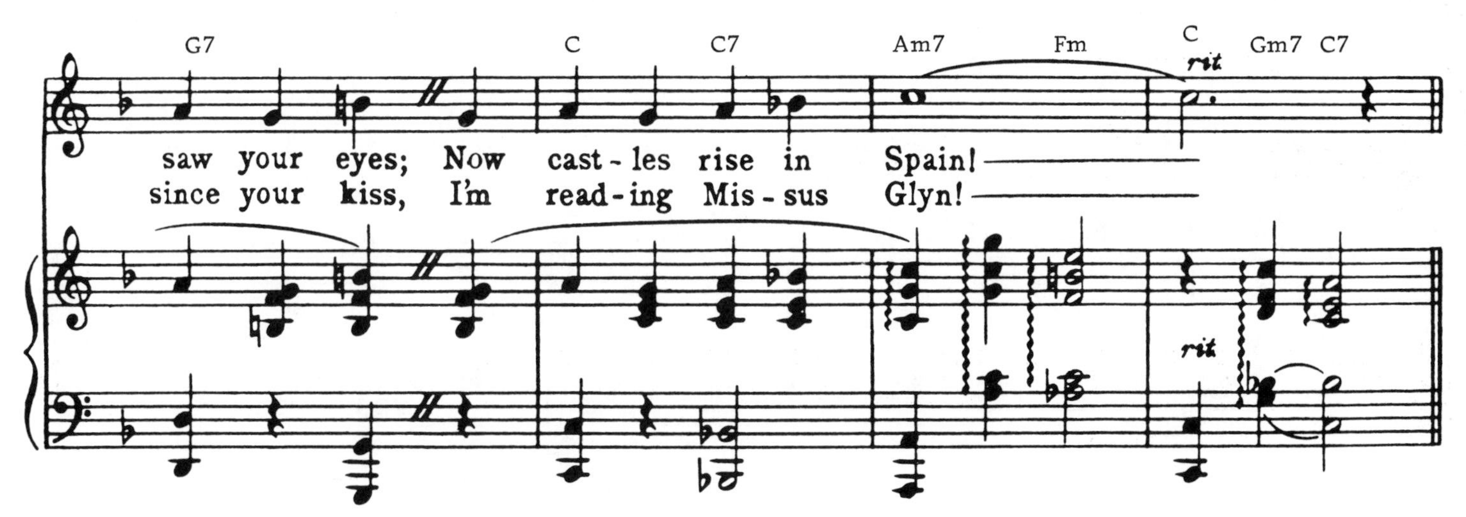
G7
C
C7
Am7
Fm
C
Gm7 C7
rit
saw your eyes; Now cast-les rise in Spain!
since your kiss, I'm read-ing Mis-sus Glyn!
rit

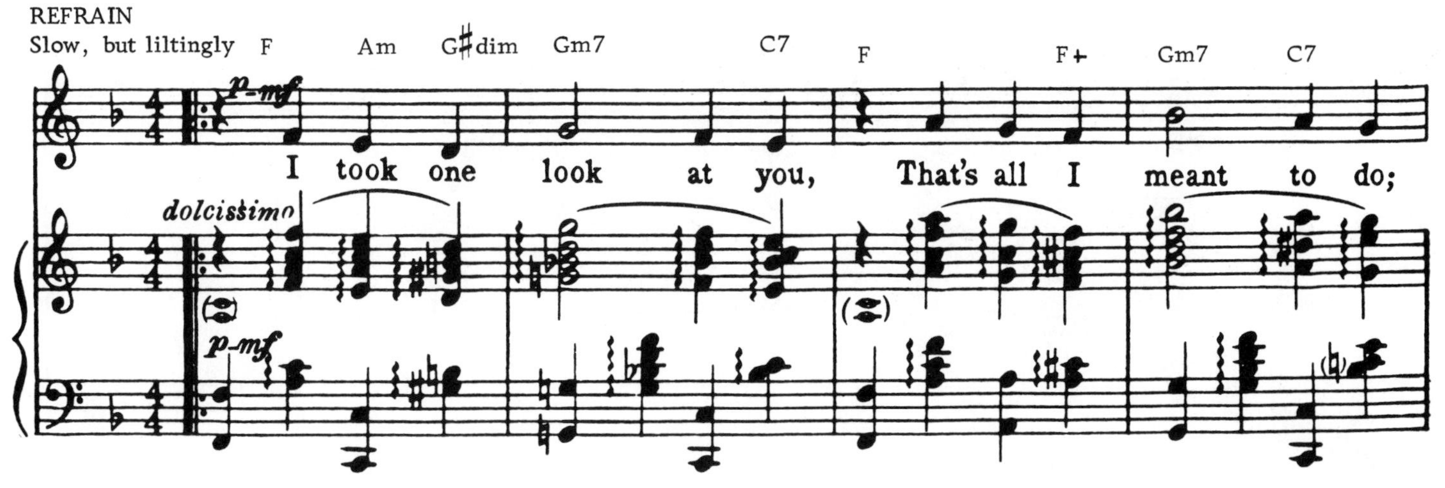
REFRAIN
Slow, but liltingly
F
Am
G♯dim
Gm7
C7
F
F+
Gm7
C7
p-mf
I took one look at you, That's all I meant to do;
dolcissimo
p-mf

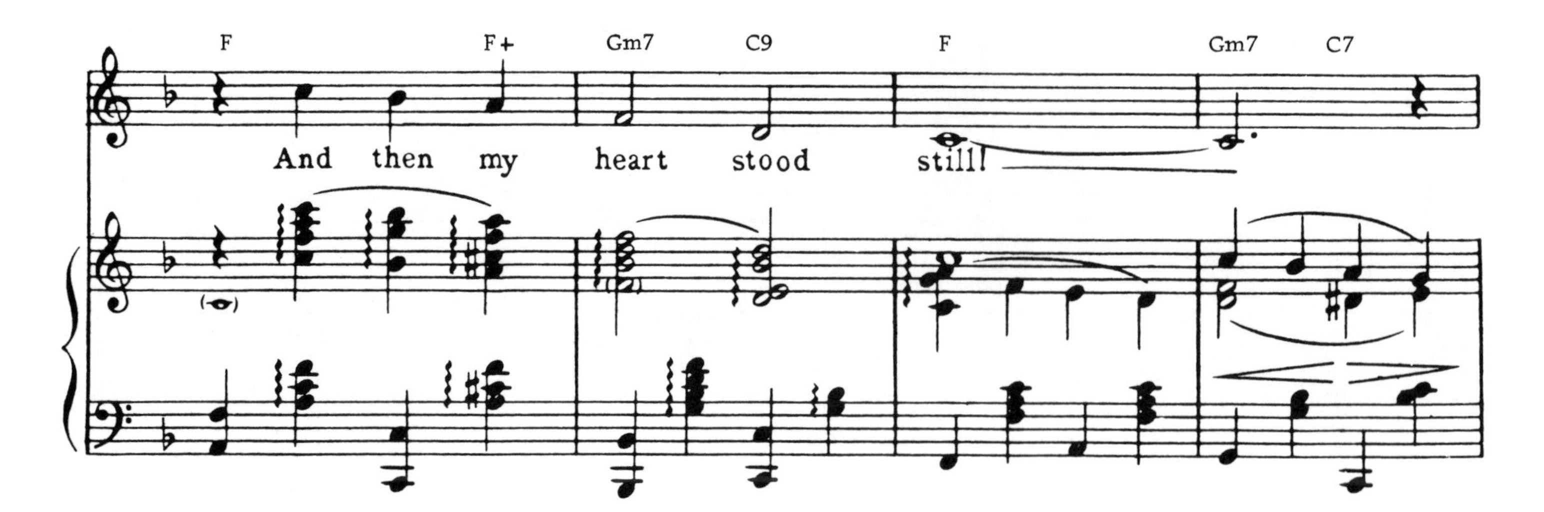
F F+ Gm7 C9 F Gm7 C7
And then my heart stood still!

F G♯dim Gm7 C7 F F+ Gm7 C7
My feet could step and walk, My lips could move and talk,
p

F F+ Gm7 C9 F B♭6 F
And yet my heart stood still! Though not a

Fm C+ C
mp
sin - gle word was spok - en, I could tell you knew,—
mp ben cantando

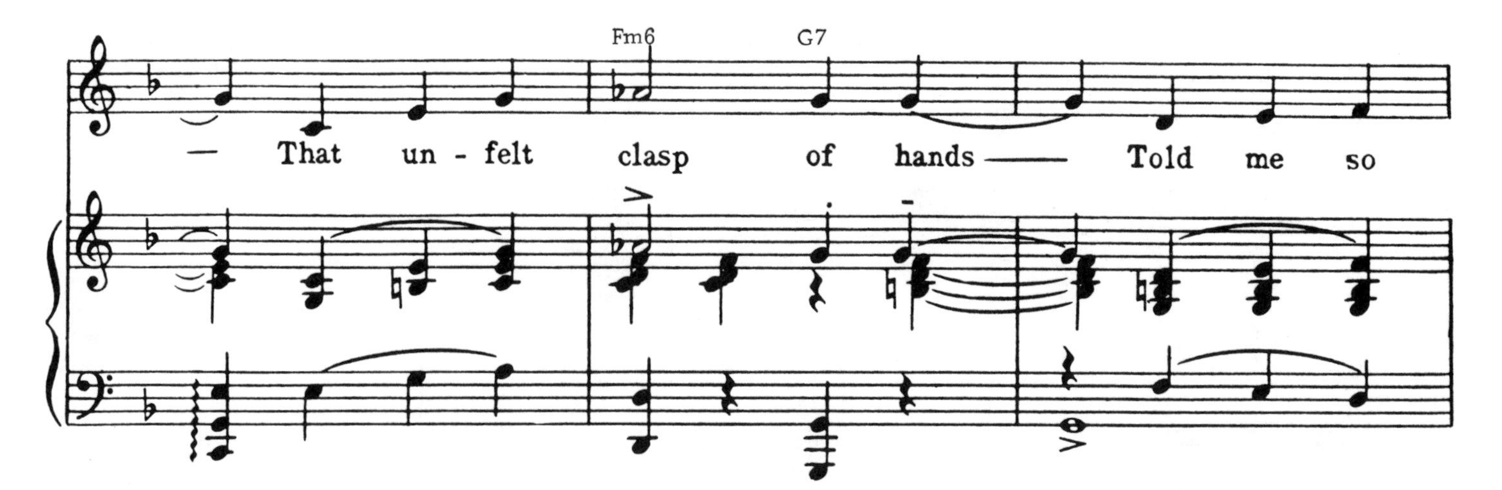
Fm6 G7
— That un - felt clasp of hands — Told me so

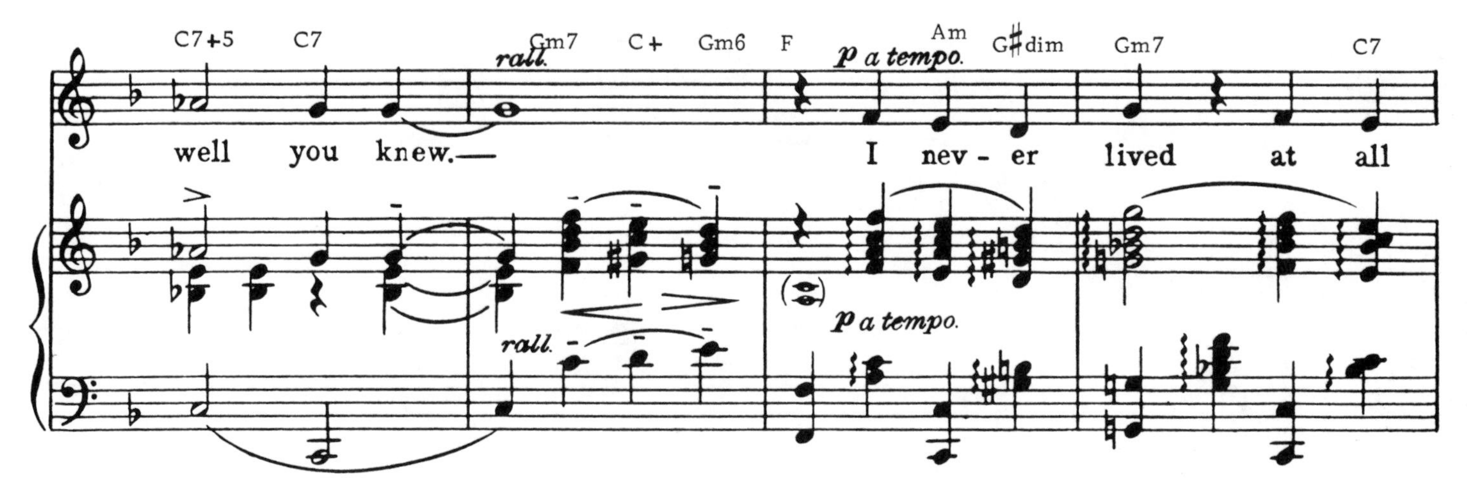
C7+5 C7 Gm7 C+ Gm6 F Am G♯dim Gm7 C7
rall.
p a tempo.
well you knew.— I nev - er lived at all

F F+ B♭ F B♭ Gm F C7
Un - til the thrill of that mo - ment when My heart stood

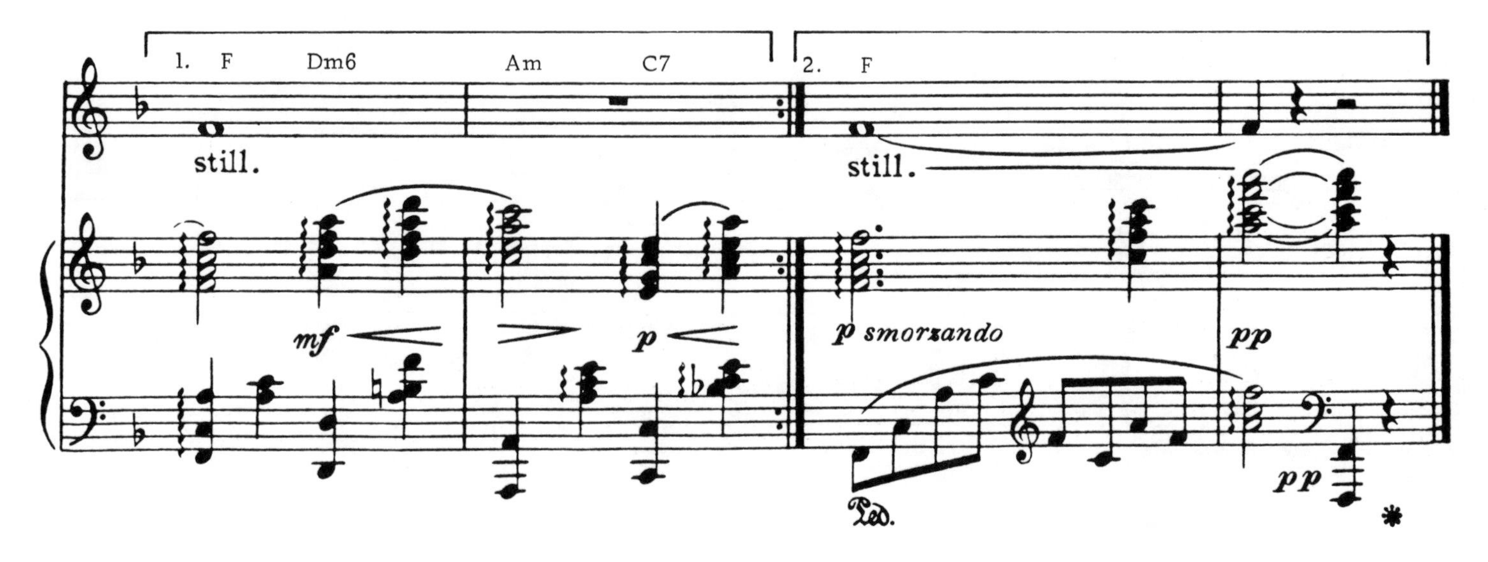
1. F Dm6 Am C7
2. F
still.
still. —
mf
p
p smorzando
pp
pp
Ped.

MY OLD FLAME

(From The Paramount Picture "BELLE OF THE NINETIES")

Words and Music by ARTHUR JOHNSTON
and SAM COSLOW

G
Bm7♭5
E7
Am
Am7
My old flame, I can't e - ven think of his
F7
D7
G6
C7
F7
B♭6
E♭7
name but it's fun - ny now and then, how my thoughts go flash - ing back a - gain, to
D
A7
Am7♭5
D7
D7♯5
G
my old flame. My old
Bm7♭5
E7
Am
Am7
F7
D7
flame, my new lov - ers all seem so tame. For I

G6 C7 F7 Bb6 Eb7 D7 A7/E
have-n't met a gent so mag - nif - i - cent or el - e - gant _ as my old
F7 Bb Am7b5 D7b9
4fr
flame. _
I've met so man - y who had fas - ci - na-tin' ways, _ a
G7#5 G7 C7sus C7
fas - ci - na - tin' gaze _ in their eyes; _
F7 D7 Gsus
some who took me up _ to the skies. _ But

A7
D7
D7#5(♭9)
4fr
G
their at-tempts at love, were on-ly im-i-ta-tions of my old
Bm7♭5
E7
Am
Am7
F7
D7
flame. I can't e-ven think of his name. But I'll
G6
C7
F7
B♭6
E♭7
3
nev-er be the same, un-til I dis-cov-er what be-came of
Am
D7#5(♭9)
4fr
1
G
Am
D7
2
G6
my old flame. flame.

MY ONE AND ONLY LOVE

Words by ROBERT MELLIN
Music by GUY WOOD

Dm7
G9
Am
Fmaj7
F6
Dm6
Em7
mys - tic charms in the hush of night while you're in my arms.
Dm7
G7
Am
F
Am
Dm7
G7
G7♭9
I feel your lips so warm and ten - der,
my one and on - ly
C
F♯m7♭5
B7
Em
F♯m7
B7
love.
The touch of your hand is like heav - en,
a
Em
F♯m7
B7
Em
Em7
heav - en that I've nev-er known.
The blush on your cheek when-

A9
Dm7
Dm7/G
G7♭9
ev - er I speak tells me that you are my own.
C
Em7
Dm7
G9
Am
Fmaj7
F6
You fill my ea - ger heart with such de - sire. Ev - 'ry kiss you give sets my
Dm6
Em7
Dm7
G7
Am
F
Am
soul on fire. I give my - self in sweet sur - ren - der,
Dm7
G7(♭9♯5)
1
C
E♭dim
Dm7
G7(♭9♯5)
2
A♭maj7
D♭6
C6/9
my one and on - ly love. love.

MY SILENT LOVE

Words by EDWARD HEYMAN
Music by DANA SUESSE

B7
B♭7
G♭
Gm
3fr
C7
turn my love a - way.
Fm6
D♭7
4fr
C7
You and I are miles a - part,
Fm
C7
Fm/A♭
C7/G
I've al - ways known it,
I just make my
Fm
C7
Fm
A♭m6
4fr
B♭7
smiles a part of the game that I must play.

Eb
3fr
Bb+
I reach for you like I'd reach for a
Eb6
Gm7b5
5fr
C7
Fm
star, wor - ship - ping you from a - far,
Abm
4fr
Bb7
Eb
3fr
Abm
4fr
Bb7#5
liv - ing with my si - lent love.
Eb
3fr
Bb+
I'm like a flame dy - ing out in the

Eb6
Gm7b5
C7
Fm
rain,
On - ly the ash - es re - main,
Abm
Bb7
Eb
Eb7
smould-'ring like my si - lent love.
Ab
Abm
Eb/Bb
no chord
How I long to tell all the things I have
Eb6
Ab
Fm7b5
planned. Still, it's wrong to tell,

F7
Bb7
Eb
3fr
You would not un - der - stand.
You'll go a -
Bb+
Eb6
Gm7b5
5fr
C7
long nev - er dream - ing I care,
lov - ing some - bod - y some -
Fm
Abm
4fr
Bb7
1
Eb
Cm7
where,
leav - ing me my si - lent love.
F7
Bb7
2
Eb
Abm
Eb
love.

THE NEARNESS OF YOU

(From The Paramount Picture "ROMANCE IN THE DARK")

Words by NED WASHINGTON
Music by HOAGY CARMICHAEL

F
Am7
Gm7
3fr
B♭/C
C7
you're at a dis - tance, but when you are near, oh
F
Fmaj7
Cm7
3fr
Cm7/F
F7♯5
my! It's not the pale moon that ex - cites me, that
B♭maj7
B♭dim7
B♭m
Am7
A♭7
4fr
thrills and de - lights me. Oh, no
Gm7
3fr
C7
Am7
A♭7
4fr
3
it's just the near - ness of you.

Gm7
C7
Fmaj7
Cm7
Cm7/F
F7♯5
It isn't your sweet con - ver - sa - tion that
B♭maj7
B♭dim7
B♭m
Am7
A♭7
brings this sen - sa - tion. Oh, no
Gm7
C7
F6
it's just the near - ness of you.
Gm7♭5
When you're in my arms

C7♭9
Fmaj7
F7
and I feel you so close to me, all my
B♭maj7
Am7♭5
D7
Gm7
3fr
E♭7
wild - est dreams come true.
C7
Fmaj7
I need no soft lights to en -
Cm7
3fr
Cm7/F
F7♯5
B♭maj7
B♭dim7
chant me if you'll on - ly grant me the

Am7
Ab7
4fr
Gm7
3fr
C7
3
right
to
hold
you
ev
-
er
so
3
Am7b5
D7b9
4fr
3
tight,
and
to
feel
in
the
3
Gm7
3fr
optional
C7
C7sus
C7
1 F
Dm7
night
the
near
-
ness
of
you.
Gm7
3fr
C7
2 F
Bb
Bbm
F6
It's
not
the
you.

ON THE SOUTH SIDE OF CHICAGO

Words and Music by
PHIL ZELLER

A9
Em7
A7
D9
The place where ac - tion first got its start back when jazz was king
G7
C
F9
C
on the south side of Chi - ca - go.
E7
Dm6/B
E7
A7
I still can hear those sil - ver trum - pets blow - in'
A9
D7
Am7
D9
In lit - tle plac - es filled with peo - ple

G9
Dm7
G9
C
glow - in'
New Or-leans was groov - y
E7
A9
Em7
A7
Mem - phis light and gay
and who could put down New York's Broad - way
But
D9
G7
C
Am
there was ev - 'ry - thing
on the south side of Chi - ca - go.
D7
G7
2
C
F9
C
B♭6
C6
ca - go.

OL' MAN RIVER
(From "SHOW BOAT")

Lyrics by OSCAR HAMMERSTEIN II
Music by JEROME KERN

Bb7 Fm7 Bb9 Eb Ab Eb D7
ol' man riv- er, he jus' keeps roll- in' a- long.
mf
Gm D7 Gm D7 Gm6 Cm Gm D7
You an' me, we sweat and strain, Bo- dy all ach- in' an' racked wid pain.
f
Gm Cm6 Gm F#dim Gm Adim Gm F7 Bb7
"Tote dat barge!" "Lift dat bale," Git a lit- tle drunk an' you land in jail.
mf
Eb Cm Eb Ab Eb Bb9 Cm F7
Ah gits wea- ry an' sick of try- in', Ah'm tired of liv- in' An' skeered of dy- in', But
f
Eb Cm Fm9 Bb7 Eb Fm7 Bb9 Eb
ol' man riv- er, he jus', keeps roll- in' a- long.
8va
mf

OUT OF NOWHERE

(From The Paramount Picture "DUDE RANCH")

Words by EDWARD HEYMAN
Music by JOHNNY GREEN

Am
E7
Am
E7
Am
E7
If it's clear or rain - ing, there is no ex -
Am
E7
A7
Em7
A7
3
plain - ing, things just hap - pen and so did
3
Am7
D7
G
you.
You came to me
Eb7
from out of no - where,

G
You took my heart and found it
Bm7
2fr
E7
Bm7
2fr
E7
Am
free.
Won - der - ful dreams,
Bm7♭5
E7
Am
won - der - ful schemes from no - where;
E♭7
3
made ev - 'ry hour sweet as a flow - er for

D7
G
me.
If you should go
Eb7
back to your no - where,
G
leav - ing me with
Bm7
E7
Bm7
E7
2fr
a mem - o - ry

Am
Bm7♭5
E7
I'll al - ways wait ___ for your re - turn out of
Am
Cm
3fr
G/B
B♭dim7
no - where; Hop - ing you'll bring your
Am7
D7
1
G
G♯dim7
Am
D7
love to me.
2
G
Cm
3fr
G
me.

PENTHOUSE SERENADE

Words and Music by WILL JASON
and VAL BURTON

Gb
Db9
But my as - pir - a - tions, I must ad - mit,
In a lit - tle while, dear; may - be I'll wait
Gdim7
Db7
Abm7/Db
Db7
4fr
G
are those of a mil - lion - aire. I can see but one place
as a nor - mal wife should do. Keep - ing the trad - i - tion,
G#dim7
D7
D7sus
that you could fit, dar - ling if you willed it,
not by the gate, but with per - am - bu - la - tor,
G7
G7#5
C6
3
I should like to build it.
by the el - e - va - tor.
Just pic - ture a pent - house way

Cdim7
Dm7
up in the sky, with hing - es on chim - neys for
G7
Dm7
G7
stars to go by; a sweet slice of heav - en for
Dm7
G7
C/E
A♭m7/E♭
Dm7
G7
just you and I when we're a - lone. From
C6
Cdim7
all of so - ci - e - ty we'll stay a - loof, and

Dm7
G7
Dm7
G7
live in pro - pri - e - ty there on the roof, two heav - en - ly her - mits we
Dm
G7
C/E
F7
G7
C
will be in truth when we're a - lone.
G7
Gdim7
G9
G9#5
3fr
We'll see life's mad pat - tern as
C
E7
Am
D7
we view old Man - hat - ten, then we can thank our

G7
Dm7
G7#5
luck - y stars, that we're liv - ing as we are. In
C6
Cdim7
Dm7
our lit - tle pent-house, we'll al - ways con - trive to keep love and ro - mance for -
G7
Dm7
G7
Dm7
G7
ev - er a - live, in view of the Hud - son just o - ver the Drive, when
1
2
C/E
B♭9
C
C#dim7
G7
C
we're a - lone. Just lone.

PUTTIN' ON THE RITZ

(From The Motion Picture "PUTTIN' ON THE RITZ")

Words and Music by
IRVING BERLIN

Dm7 G7 C6 C♯dim Dm7 G7
Ar - row col - lars, white spats and lots of dol - lars,
Am Am7 D7 G7 C7♭9 C7♯5 C7
spend - ing ev - 'ry dime for a won-der-ful time.
Fm
If you're blue and you don't know where to go to, why don't you
C7 C7♭9
go where fash - ion sits, put - tin' on the

Fm
Fm/E♭
D♭9
C7
Fm
Ritz.
Diff-'rent types who wear _ a day coat, pants
C7
C7♭9
with stripes and cut - a - way coat, per - fect fits, ___
Fm
Fm/E♭
D♭
F7/C
B♭m
___ put - tin' on the Ritz.
Strol - ling up the
(Alt: Dressed up like a
G♭9
F9
B♭m6
E♭9
E♭7♯5
E♭7
A♭6
Fm7
a - ve - nue so hap - py. ___
mil - lion dol - lar troup - er. ___
All dressed up just
Try - ing hard to

B♭m7
E♭7
A♭6
D♭9
C9
like an Eng - lish chap - pie, __ ve - ry snap - py.
look like Gar - y Coo - per, __ su - per du - per.)
Fm
Come let's mix where Rock - e - fel - lers walk with sticks or "um - ber -
C7
C7♭9
el - las" in their mitts, __ put - tin' on the
1
Fm
D♭7
C7♭9
C9
Ritz. __
2
Fm
B♭m6
F6/9
Ritz. __

ROCKIN' CHAIR

Words and Music by
HOAGY CARMICHAEL

E♭
B♭7+5
E♭
Fm7
E♭
Hear't no more.
mp
G7 G7+5 A♭m6 G7
Bdim Cm6 D7-5 G7
E♭aug Bm6
Cm
Years have slipped a - way and left me long - in'
F9 Dm
F7
B♭ F7
B♭7 Gm D B♭7
For the days of hap - pi - ness I'll see no more.
Refrain
E♭
E♭9
A♭
A♭m
Old Rock - in' Chair's got me, cane by my side,
mp mf

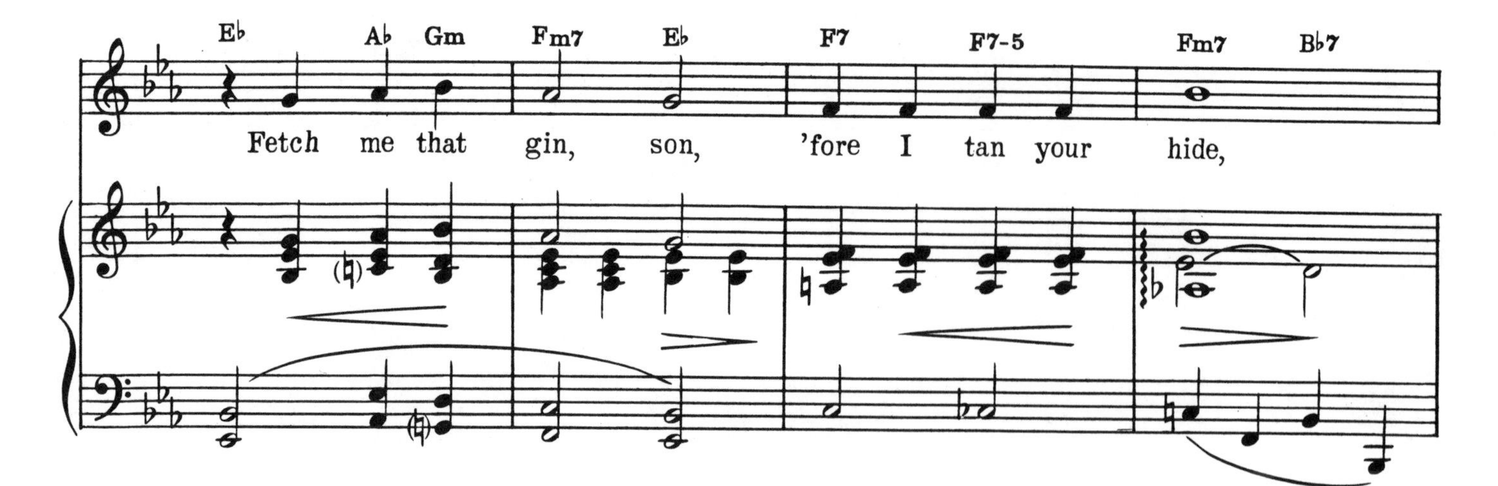
E♭ A♭ Gm Fm7 E♭ F7 F7-5 Fm7 B♭7
Fetch me that gin, son, 'fore I tan your hide,

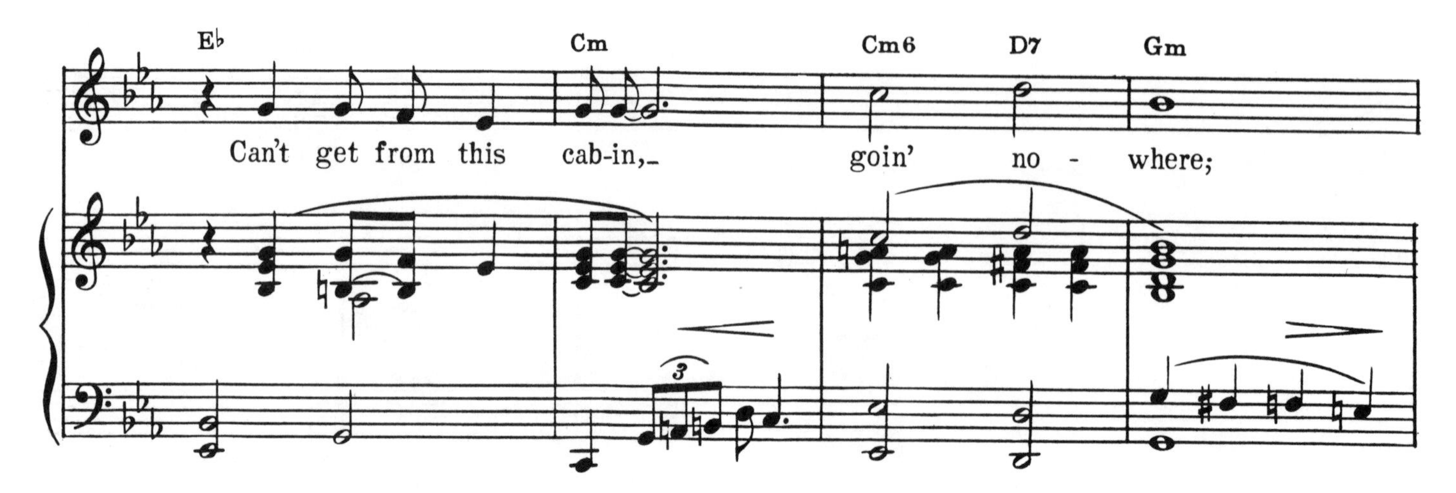
E♭ Cm Cm6 D7 Gm
Can't get from this cab-in, goin' no - where;
3

F7 Dm F7 E♭ F♯m Gm
Just sit me here grab - bin' at the flies 'round this Rock - in'

E♭ A♭9 E♭ Gm
Chair. My dear old Aunt Har - ri - et in hea-ven she

E♭
Am7-5 D7
Gm
Gm6
be, Send me sweet cha-ri-ot, for the
Cm7
F9
B♭7 sus. E♭ B♭7
B♭9
E♭
E♭9
end of these trou-ble I see. Old Rock- in' Chair gits it,
mp mf
A♭
A♭m
E♭
A♭m C7
F7 F♭
Judg-ment day is here, Chained to my Rock - in'
1.
2.
E♭
Fm7
Gm B♭7+5
E♭ A♭9
E♭6
Chair.
Chair.

SIDE BY SIDE

Words and Music by
HARRY WOODS

F7
some - bod - y feels a - bout me We're sure we love each
soon as we've giv - en our vow But we'd all be so
B♭
F7
B♭ B♭dim B♭7
oth - er That's the way we'll al - ways be:
hap - py If we'd start and sing right now:
E♭
A♭
E♭
Oh! we ain't got a bar - rel of mon - ey, May - be we're rag - ged and
p-f

A♭
E♭
A♭
E♭
C7
fun - ny, But we'll trav - el a - long Sing - in' a song

F7 B♭7 E♭ A♭ E♭
Side By Side Don't know what's com - in' to - mor - row,
A♭ E♭ A♭
May - be it's trou - ble and sor - row, But we'll trav - el the road,
E♭ C7 F7 B♭7 E♭ G7+5
Sha - rin' our load Side By Side. Thru all kinds of
G7 C7 F7
wea - ther What if the sky should fall Just as long as we're to -

B♭7
B♭dim
B♭7
gether, It does - n't mat - ter at all When they've
E♭
A♭
E♭
all had their quar - rels and part - ed We'll be the same as we
A♭
E♭
A♭
E♭
C7
start - ed Just trav - 'lin' a - long Sing - in' a song
F7
B♭7
1 E♭
2 E♭
Side By Side. Oh! we Side.
fz

SING, YOU SINNERS

(From The Paramount Picture "HONEY")

Words and Music by SAM COSLOW
and W. FRANKE HARLING

Dm/F
Em7♭5
A7
B♭
A7
Dm
A7
vo - de - o - do and sing all your trou - bles a - way.
rall.
Slowly
Dm
G
Dm
Broth - ers ___ and sis - ters, ___ don't you ___ de -

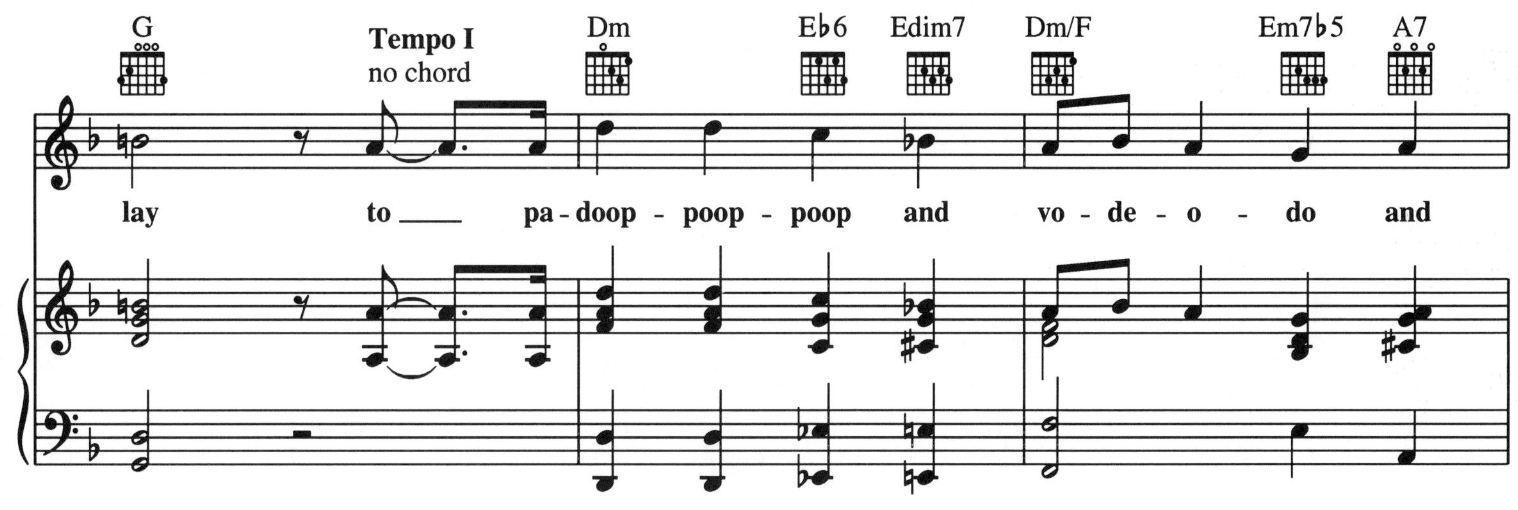
G
Tempo I
no chord
Dm
E♭6
Edim7
Dm/F
Em7♭5
A7
lay to ___ pa - doop - poop - poop and vo - de - o - do and

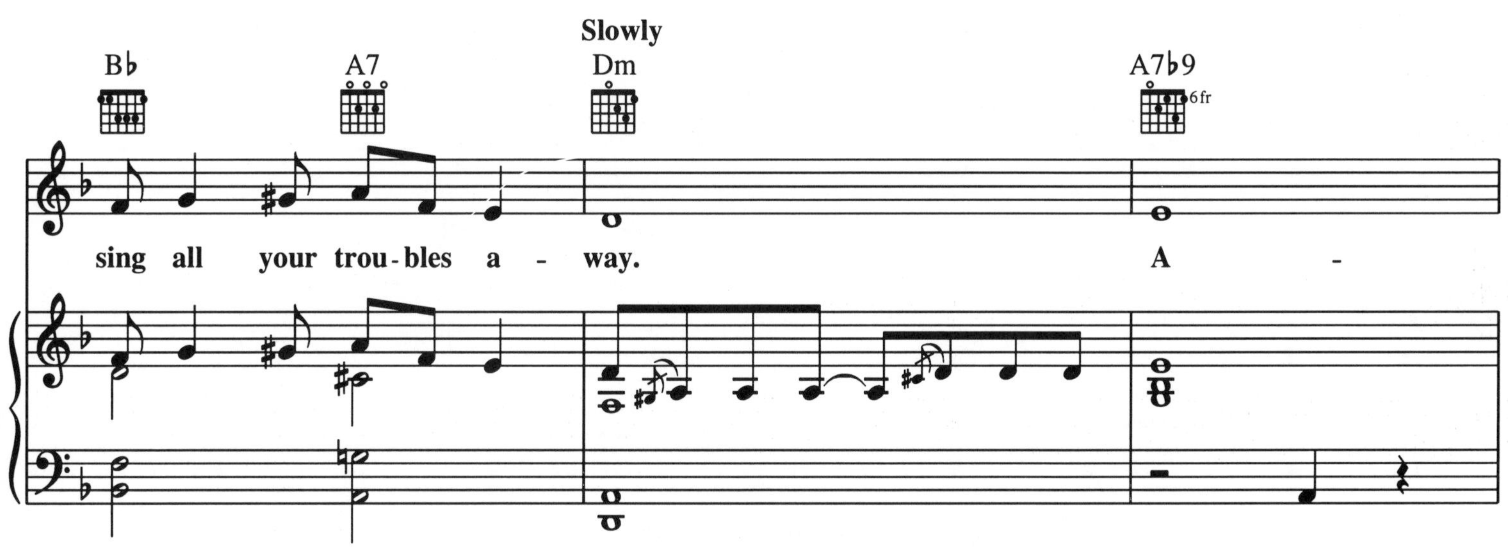
B♭
A7
Slowly
Dm
A7♭9
6fr
sing all your trou - bles a - way. A -

Moderately
Dm
A7♭9
6fr
Dm F Dm
men, A - men! You sin - ners,
F Dm/C F Dm/C Fm B♭9
drop ev - 'ry-thing. Let dat har-mo - ny ring
Fm6 B♭9 F/C C7♯5
up to heav-en and sing, sing, you
F
no chord
F Dm/C
sin - ners. Just wave your arms all a-bout.

F Dm/C Fm B♭9 Fm6 B♭9
Let the Lord hear you shout. Pour dat
F/C C7♯5 F6 F
mu - sic right out. Sing, you sin - ners. __

A/E F+ A7 Dm Gm
3fr
When - ev - er there's mu - sic

A Dm B♭7 Dm
the deb - il kicks. __ He don't al - low

Gm
G7
C7
no chord
mu - sic by dat riv - er Styx. You're wick - ed
F
Dm/C
F
Dm/C
Fm
B♭9
and you're de-praved and you've all mis - be-haved.
Fm6
B♭9
F/C
C7♯5
If you wan - na be saved, sing, you
F
1
C7♯5
no chord
2
C7♯5
F
sin - ners. You sin - ners,

SPANISH EYES

Words by CHARLES SINGLETON and EDDIE SNYDER
Music by BERT KAEMPFERT

please don't cry.
Span - ish eyes,
This is just a -
please smile for me once
G
dios and not good - bye.
more be - fore I go.
Soon
I'll re - turn,
bring - ing you all the
G7
C
Cm
love your heart can hold.
Please

Cm6
G
say Si Si.
Say
D7
G
you and your Span - ish eyes will wait for me.
A♭
4fr
Span - ish eyes,
wait for me, say Si
G
A♭
4fr
G
Si!

264
SPEAK SOFTLY, LOVE
(LOVE THEME)
(From The Paramount Picture "THE GODFATHER")
Words by LARRY KUSIK
Music by NINO ROTA
Slowly
Cm Fm6/C Cm Fm6/C Cm Fm6/C
mp
Cm Fm6/C Cm Fm/C Cm
Speak soft - ly, love, and hold me warm a-gainst your heart. I feel your
Cm/E♭ Fm
words, the ten-der, trem-bling mo-ments start. We're in a world our ver - y
Cm Cm/G G7sus G7 Cm
own, shar-ing a love that on - ly few have ev - er known. Wine col-ored

B♭7/D
B♭7
E♭
3fr
D♭/F
Fm6/A♭
6fr
days warmed by the sun, deep vel-vet nights when we are
G
no chord
Cm
3fr
Fm/C
Cm
3fr
one. Speak soft-ly, love, so no one hears us but the sky. The vows of
Fm/C
Cm
3fr
Fm6/C
6fr
Cm
3fr
Fm/C
Fm
love we make will live un-til we die. My life is yours and all be-
Cm
3fr
Cm/G
3fr
G7sus
G7
1
Cm
3fr
2
Cm
3fr
cause you came in-to my world with love so soft-ly, love. Speak soft-ly, love.
rit.

STELLA BY STARLIGHT

(From The Paramount Picture "THE UNINVITED")

Words by NED WASHINGTON
Music by VICTOR YOUNG

G/B
E♭7/B♭
Am7
D7
G/D
when have you known rap - ture so rare? The
C♯m7♭5
2fr
F♯7
Am7
song a rob - in sings
D7♯5
D7
Dm9/G
G7♭9
4fr
through years of end - less
Cmaj9
F13
G/D
springs. The mur - mur of a

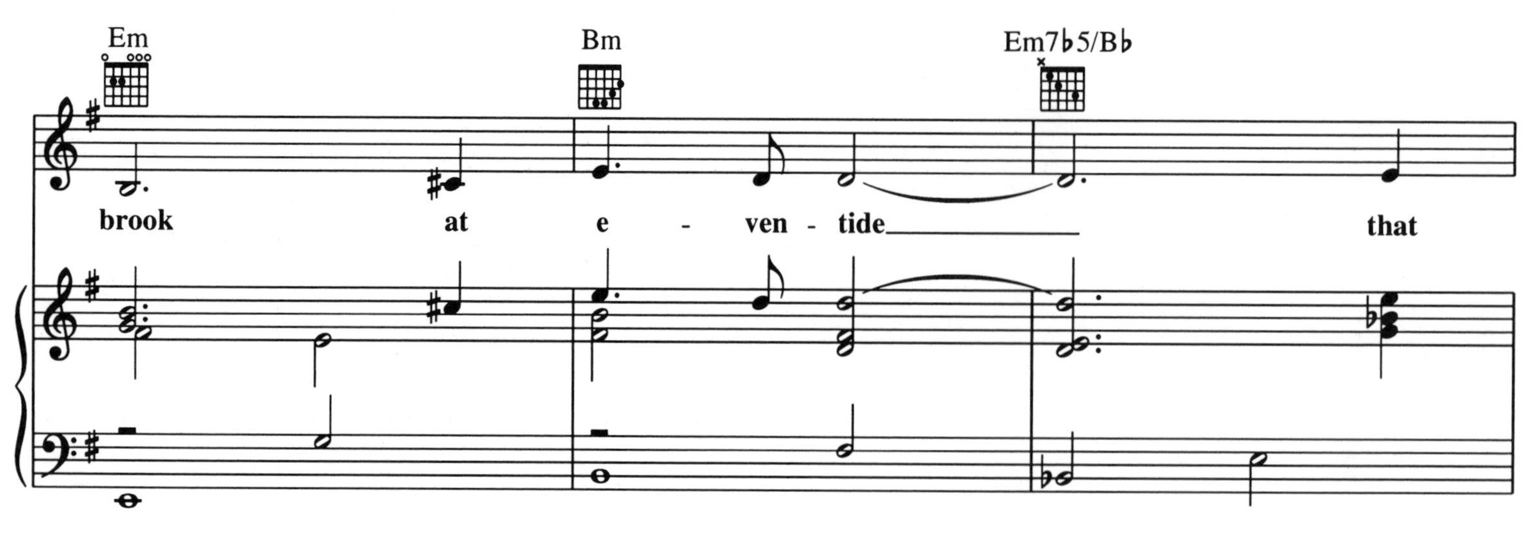
Em
Bm
Em7♭5/B♭
brook at e - ven - tide that

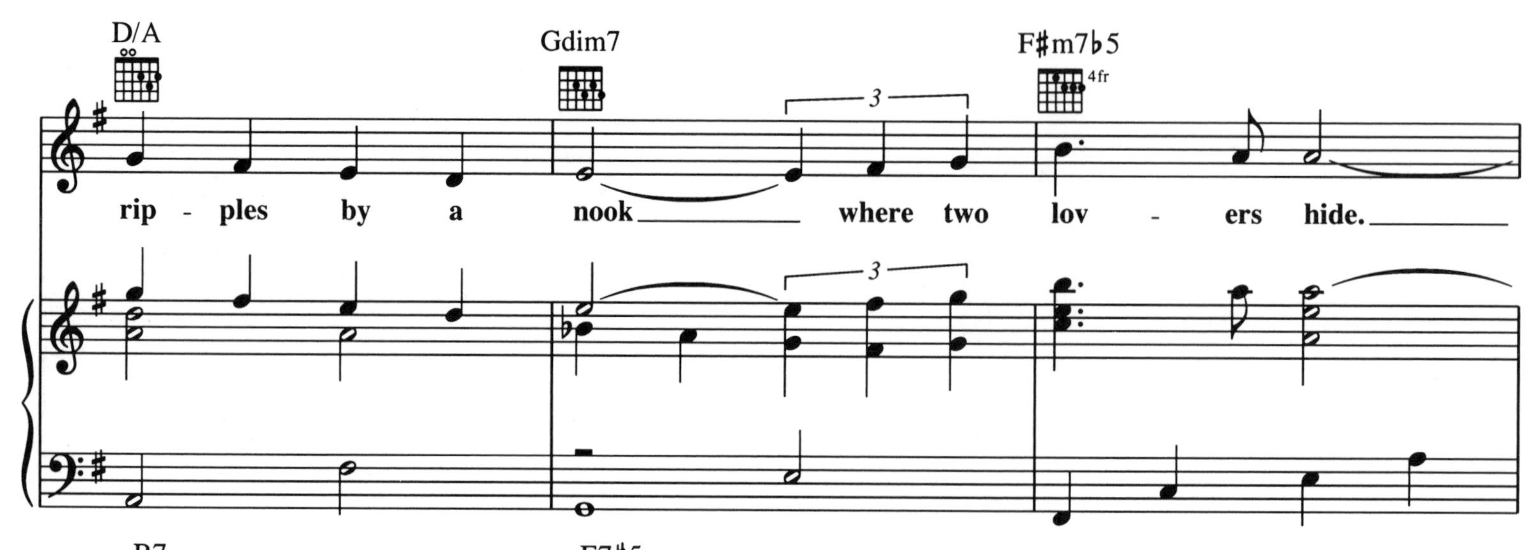
D/A
Gdim7
F♯m7♭5
4fr
3
rip - ples by a nook where two lov - ers hide.

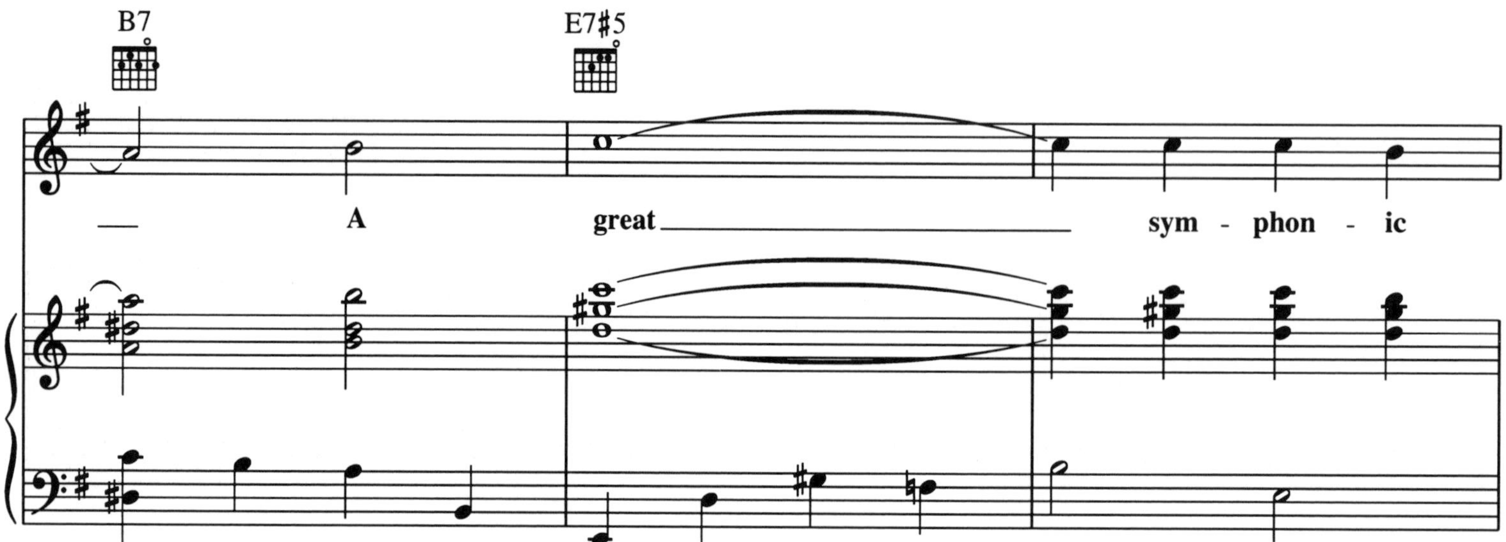
B7
E7♯5
A great sym - phon - ic

Am
Cm
3fr
3
theme, that's Stel - la by star - light

G6/9
and not a dream.
(Boy): My
(Girl): She's
C#m7♭5
F#7
Bm7♭5
heart and I a - gree
all of these and more
E7
Am7♭5
she's ev - 'ry - thing
she's ev - 'ry - thing
D7
G(add9)
on earth to me.
that you'd a - dore.

STAR DUST

Words by MITCHELL PARISH
Music by HOAGY CARMICHAEL

G7 G7+5 C C6
and each kiss an in - spir - a - tion, But
D7 C D7 G7 Dm7
that was long a - go: now my con - so - la - tion is in the star dust of a
G7 Gdim G7 C7+5 F6 Fm6
song. Be - side a gar - den wall, when stars are bright,
C Em A7
you are in my arms, The night - in - gale tells his fair - y tale

Dm7 A7 Dm7 Fm6 Dm7-5
of par - a - dise, where ros - es grew. Tho' I dream in vain.
Fm C G Am C B7 B7-5 E7 E7+5
In my heart it will re - main: My
F6 A7 Adim G7 1 C Ab7
star dust mel - o - dy, The mem - o - ry of love's re - frain.
3
Fm6 G7 C7+5 2 C C6 Cm Cmaj7 C6
Some - times I frain.

THAT'S AMORE

(THAT'S LOVE)

(From The Paramount Picture "THE CADDY")

Words by JACK BROOKS
Music by HARRY WARREN

F7/C
Bdim7
Cm7
3fr
F7
mor - é.
When the
world seems to shine like you've had too much wine, that's a -
B♭
mor - é.
Bells will
B♭/D
D♭dim7
ring, ting - a - ling - a - ling, ting - a - ling - a - ling, and you'll sing, "Vee - ta

F7/C
Bdim7
F7/C
F7
3fr
3fr
bel - la."
Hearts will
a tempo
play, tip - py - tip - py - tay, tip - py - tip - py - tay like a gay tar - an -
B♭
(Optional)
tel - la. (Luck - y fel - la.) When the
3
3
B♭/D
D♭dim7
stars make you drool just like pas - ta fa - zool, that's a -

F7/C
Bdim7
Cm7
F7
3 fr
mor - é.
When you
dance down the street with a cloud at your feet, you're in
D7/A
A♭7♭5
G7
love.
When you
Cm
Eb♭m6
walk in a dream but you know you're not dream - ing, Sig -

B♭
D♭dim7
nor - é, scuz - za
F7/C D♭dim7 F7/C D♭dim7 F7/C F7
me, but you see, back in old Na - po - li, that's a -
1
B♭ E♭6/B♭ B♭maj7 Cm7 F7
mor - é. When the
2
B♭ E♭m6/B♭ B♭
mor - é.

TANGERINE

(From The Paramount Picture "THE FLEET'S IN")

Words by JOHNNY MERCER
Music by VICTOR SCHERTZINGER

A/E
Bm
E7
Em7/A
A7
D7#5
treme, wait till you see her face. Tan - ge -
Gm7
C7
F6
rine, she is all they claim,
F6/A
A♭dim7
Gm7
C7
Gm7
C7
with her eyes of night and lips as bright as
F
D7#5
Gm7
flame. Tan - ge - rine,

C7
F6
E7
when she danc - es by Señ - or -
A
F♯m7
Bm7
2 fr
E7
A7
i - tas stare and ca - bal - le - ros sigh.
D7
D7♯5
Gm7
3 fr
C7
F6
And I've seen toasts to Tan - ge - rine
F6/A
A♭dim7
4 fr
Gm7
3 fr
C7
Gm7
3 fr
C7
raised in ev - 'ry bar a - cross the Ar - gen -

A7
D7
D7♯5
D7
Gm
3fr
Gm/F
tine. Yes, she has them all on the
Em7
A7
Dm7
F/G
G7
run but her heart be - longs to just one. Her
B♭
Gm7
3fr
Gm7/C
C7
1
F
Cm/E♭
3fr
heart be - longs to Tan - ge - rine.
D7
D7♯5
2
F
Tan - ge - rine.
rit.

THANKS FOR THE MEMORY

(From The Paramount Picture "BIG BROADCAST OF 1938")

Words and Music by LEO ROBIN
and RALPH RAINGER

Bb6
Bbm6/Db
C7
C13
love - ly it was! Thanks for the
love - ly it was! Thanks for the
F6
F#dim7
mem - o - ry of rain - y af - ter - noons, __
mem - o - ry of lin - ge - rie with lace, __
C7/G
F/A
D#dim7
C7/E
swing - y Har - lem tunes, __ and mo - tor trips and burn - ing lips and
Pils - ner by the case, __ and how I jumped the day you trumped my
F#dim7
Gm7
Adim7
Bb6
burn - ing toast and prunes. __ How love - ly it
one and on - ly ace. __ How love - ly it

B♭m6/D♭
C7
E♭7
A♭
E♭9
was! Man-y's the time that we feast-ed and
was! We said good-bye with a high-ball; then
A♭
Adim7
C/G
Am
man-y's the time that we fast-ed. Oh, well, it was swell while it
I got as "high" as a stee-ple. But we were in-tel-li-gent
Dm
Fm6/C
G7
Gm7
Gm7♭5
C7
C+
D♭dim7
last-ed; we did have fun and no harm done. And
peo-ple; no tears, no fuss, hur-ray for us. So
a tempo
C13
F6
F♯dim7
thanks for the mem-o-ry of sun-burns at the shore,
thanks for the mem-o-ry and strict-ly en-tre-nous,

C7/G
F/A
D♯dim7
C7/E
nights in Sing - a - pore.
You might have been a head - ache but you
dar - ling, how are you?
And how are all the lit - tle dreams that
1
F♯dim7
Gm7
Adim7
B♭6
C7
F
C7♯5
C7
nev - er were a bore,
so thank you so much.
2
F♯dim7
Gm7
G♯dim7
F/A
nev - er did come true?
Awf - 'ly glad I met you, chee - ri -
D♭7/A♭
Gm7
C7
D♭
F6
o and too - dle - oo and thank you so much!

THAT OLD BLACK MAGIC

(From The Paramount Picture "STAR SPANGLED RHYTHM")

Words by JOHNNY MERCER
Music by HAROLD ARLEN

Moderately

Eb6

p

Eb

That old black magic has me in its spell. That old black magic that you weave so well. Those

Fm/Eb

i - cy fin - gers up and down my spine. The
B♭9♯5/E♭
E♭6
B♭9♯5
4fr
same old witch - craft when your eyes meet mine. The
E♭
3fr
same old tin - gle that I feel in - side,
cresc. poco a poco
and then that el - e - va - tor starts its ride,
D♭
D♭7
4fr
rit.
f a tempo

A♭6
A♭m6
E♭maj9
and down and down I go, 'round and 'round
dim. poco a poco
C+
Fm7
Emaj7
E♭
I go like a leaf that's caught in the tide.
p
Cm
A♭9♯11
I should stay a-way but what can I do?
mf
G9
C9
I hear your name and I'm a-flame,

Fm
a - flame with such a burn - ing de -
Db9
Abm6
sire that on - ly your kiss
Bb13
can put out the fire. For
Eb
you're the lov - er I have wait - ed for,
pp
p

B♭m7/E♭
6fr
the mate that fate had me cre - at - ed for, and ev - 'ry time your lips meet mine, dar - ling, down and down I go, 'round and 'round
cresc. poco a poco
E♭9
A♭
4fr
f
A♭m6
4fr
A♭6/9
A♭m6
4fr
E♭maj7
3fr
dim.
p

C+
Fm7/E♭
I go in a spin, lov - ing the
Fm7♭5/E♭
6fr
B♭7sus/E♭
6fr
spin I'm in, un - der that old black mag -
rit.
1
E♭6
2
E♭6
- ic called love! That love!
a tempo
a tempo
Fm7♭5/E♭
6fr
E♭6/9
rit. e dim.
pp

THAT'S LIFE

Words and Music by DEAN KAY
and KELLY GORDON

A9
Am7
D9
G
B7
back on top in June. THAT'S LIFE, Fun-ny as it seems,

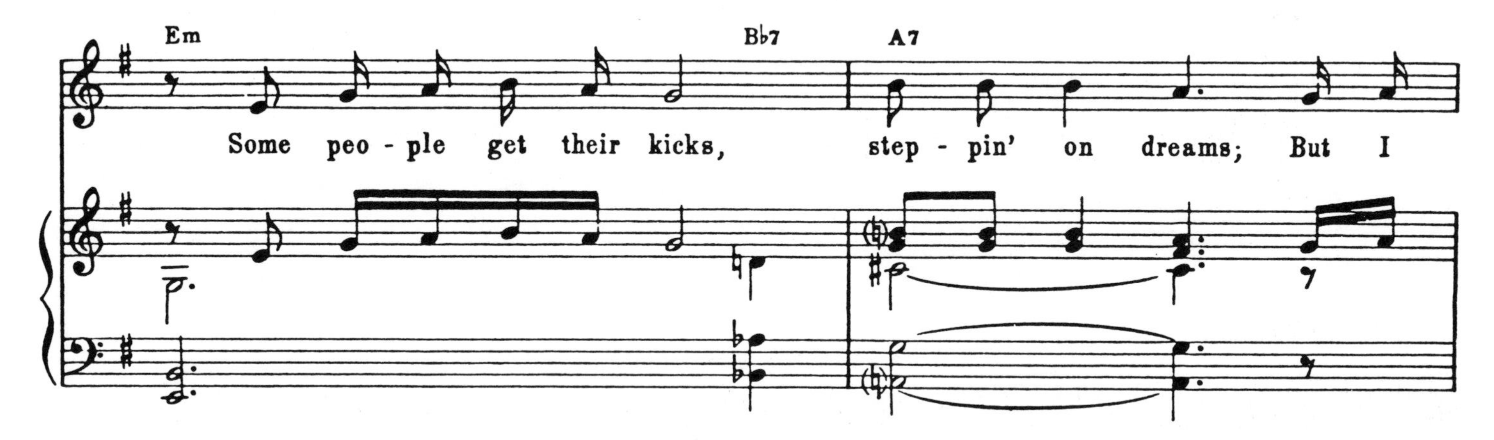
Em
B♭7
A7
Some peo-ple get their kicks, step-pin' on dreams; But I

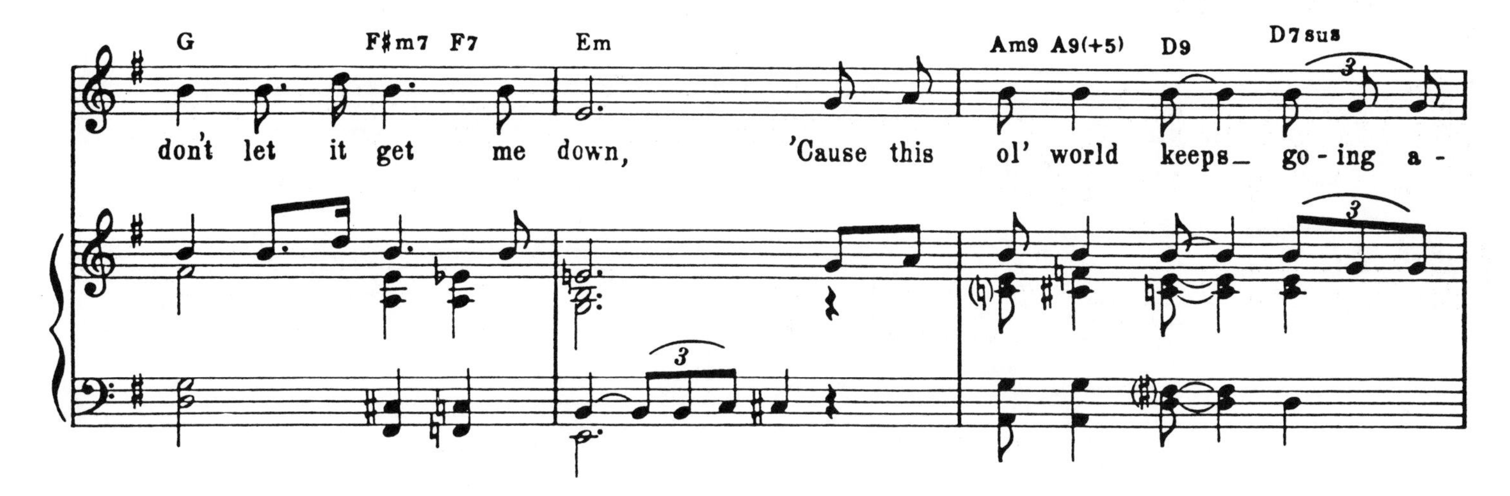
G
F♯m7
F7
Em
Am9
A9(+5)
D9
D7sus
don't let it get me down, 'Cause this ol' world keeps_ go-ing a-

G
G7
round. I've been a pup-pet, a pau-per, a pi-rate, a po-et, a

G7
C6
pawn and a king._ I've been up and down and o - ver and out And

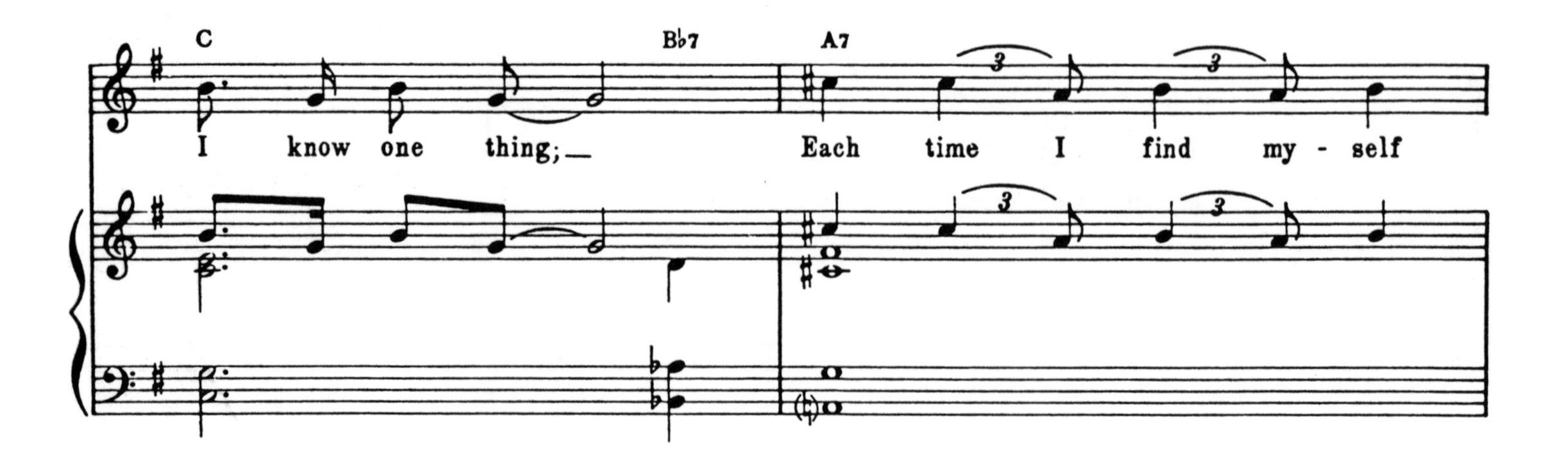
C
Bb7
A7
I know one thing;_ Each time I find my - self

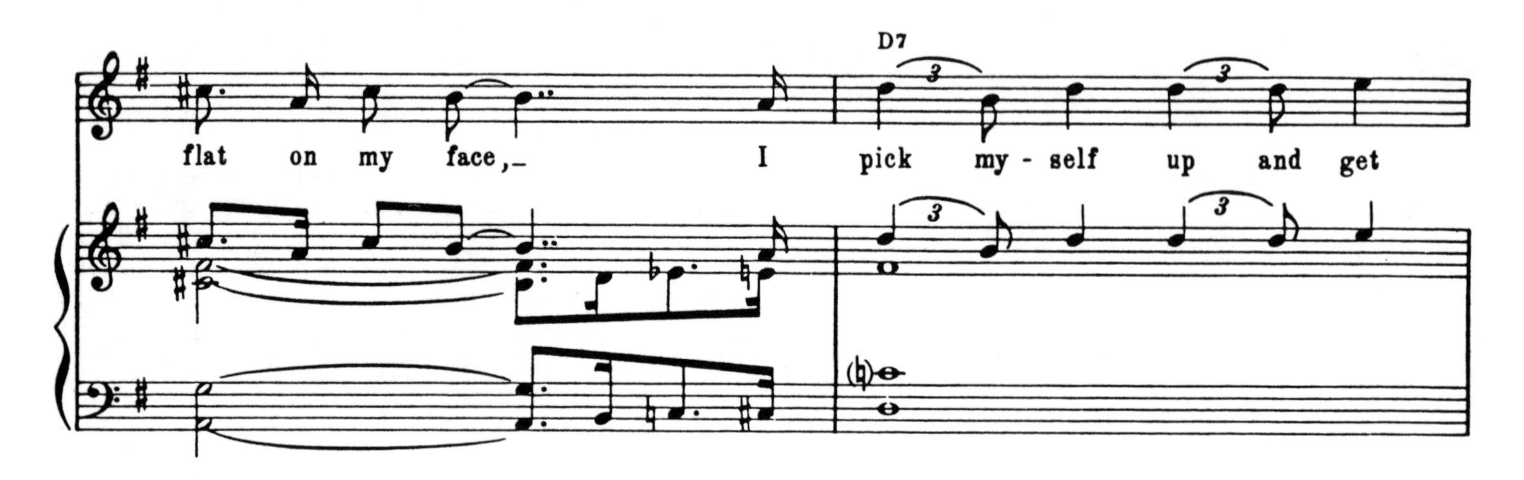
D7
flat on my face,_ I pick my - self up and get

D7
D9(+5)
G
B7
back in the race._ THAT'S LIFE, I can't de - ny it,

Em
I thought of quit - ting, but my heart just won't buy it. If I
A7
Cm6
rit.

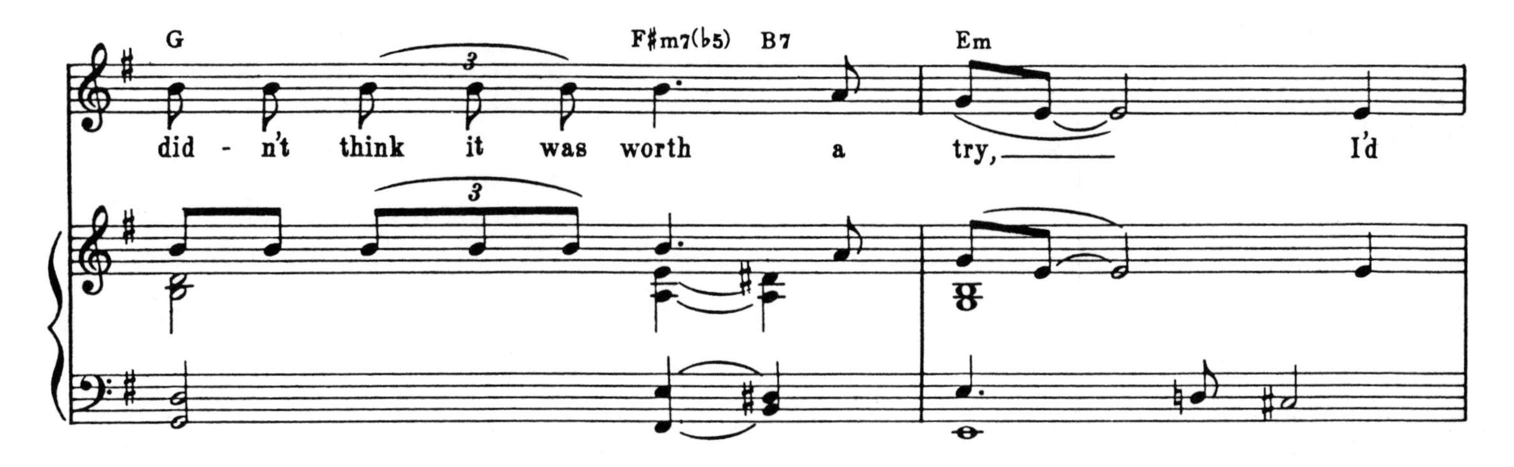
G
F#m7(♭5) B7
Em
did - n't think it was worth a try,
I'd

A7(♭9)
D7
1. G
F9
A7(+5)
D9
roll my-self up in a big ball and die.
THAT'S

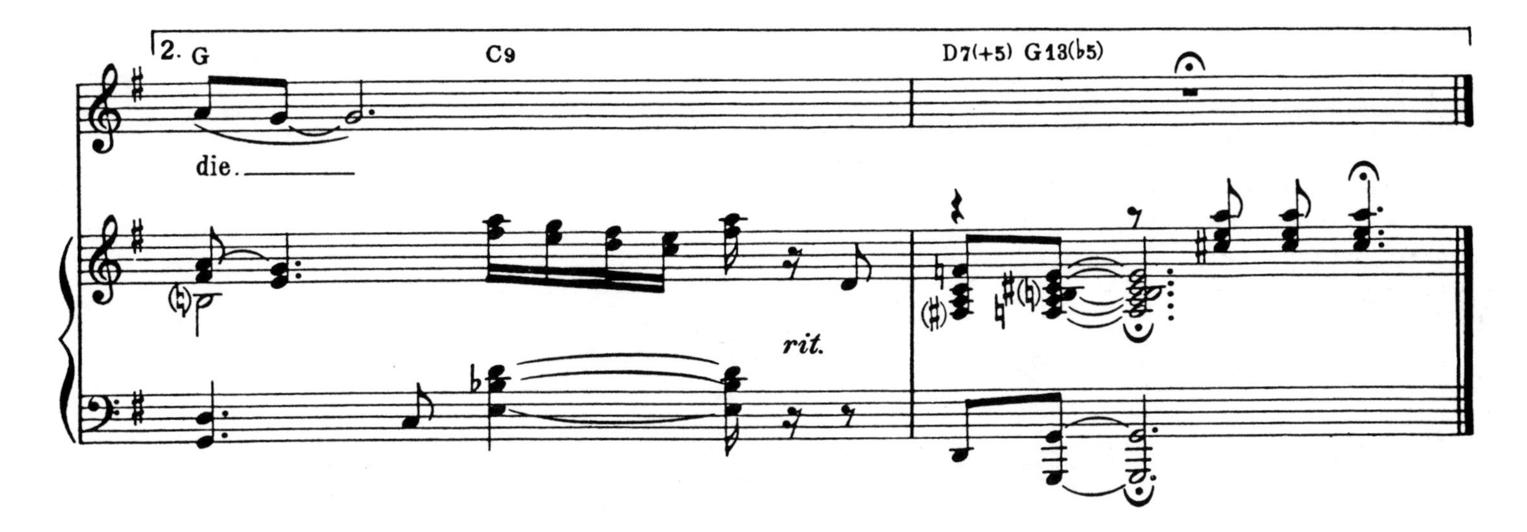
2. G
C9
D7(+5) G13(♭5)
die.
rit.

THEY SAY IT'S WONDERFUL

(From The Stage Production "ANNIE GET YOUR GUN")

Words and Music by
IRVING BERLIN

Gm7
Gm7♭5
set my heart a - glow.
heard is real - ly so.
F6/A
Dm7
Gm7
G♭7
F
Wish I knew if the things I hear are so.
I've been there once or twice and I should know.
F/A
D♭9/A♭
Slowly
Gm7
B♭m6/D♭
C7
(Annie:) They say that fall - ing in love is
(Frank:) You'll find that fall - ing in love is
rall.
mf
a tempo
F/A
A♭dim7
Gm7♭5
C7♭9
C7
won - der - ful, it's won - der - ful so they
won - der - ful, it's won - der - ful (Annie:) so you

F(add9)
F♯dim
Gm7
B♭m6/D♭
C7
say. And with a moon up a - bove, it's
say. (Frank:) And with a moon up a - bove, it's
F/A
A♭dim
Gm7♭5
C7♭9
C7
won - der - ful, it's won - der - ful so they
won - der - ful, it's won - der - ful (Annie:) so you
F7
F9♭5
F9
F7♯5/E♭
B♭
B♭m♯7
tell me. I can't re - call who said it, I
tell me. (Frank:) To leave your house some morn - ing, and
F/A
Am
know I nev - er read it. I on - ly know they
with - out an - y warn - ing, you're stop - ping peo - ple

G♯dim
E7
Am
A♭m6
Gm7
tell me that love is grand, and the thing that's
shout - ing that love is grand. And to hold a
B♭m6/D♭
C7
Am7
D7♯5♭9
D7
known as ro - mance is won - der - ful, won - der - ful
man in your arms is won - der - ful, won - der - ful
G7sus
G9
Gm7
G♭7♭5
F6
Dm9
in ev - 'ry way, so they say.
in ev - 'ry way, (Annie:) so you
Gm9
F/A
A♭m6
F6
Dm7
Gm7
G♭7
F6
say.

THOU SWELL

(From "A CONNECTICUT YANKEE")

Words by LORENZ HART
Music by RICHARD RODGERS

Fm7 Bb9 Eb D7 Fm7 Bb+5 Eb6 E♮dim
Are you too wist - full to care,- Do — say you — care to —
More thou wilt tell to San - dy. — Thou — art dan - dy; Now —
Fm6 Bb7 Eb Eb6 Eb Gm Cm
dim.
— say; "Come near lad." You are so grace - ful,
— art thou my knight. Thine arms are mar - tial;
dim.
poco scherzando
D7 Gm Eb Cm D7 Gm
have you wings? You have a face full of nice things;
Thou hast grace; My cheek is part - ial to thy face;
Cm F7 Bb6 Cm Cm7 F7 Bb7
You have no speak - ing voice, dear, With ev - 'ry word it sings. —
And if thy lips grow wea - ry, Mine are their rest - ing place. —
rall.
rit

F9
Bb7
Slow with grace
Thou swell! Thou wit ty! Thou sweet! Thou grand! Wouldst
kiss me pret-ty? Wouldst hold my hand? Both thine eyes are cute too;
What they do to me. Hear me hol-ler I choose a Sweet
lol-la-pa-loo-sa in thee. I'd feel so
Eb6
Bb9
Eb
A dim
C
F
Bb
+5
Ab6
G7
Cm7
C7
Gm
D7 b5
mf
dim.
mp
p

5
Bb7
F9
Bb7
F9
Bb7
Eb6
Bb9
Eb6
Bb9
rich in a hut for two; Two rooms and kit-chen I'm
Eb6
Bb9
Eb
Ebdim
Bb7
C
Fm
Bb
sure would do; Give me just a plot of, Not a lot of
mf
G7
C+
C7
F7
F9
Bb7
land And Thou swell! Thou wit-ty! Thou
1. Eb
F#dim
Bb7
F9
2. Eb
Fm6
Cm7
Bb7
Eb
grand! Thou grand!
mf
mf
sf

TWO SLEEPY PEOPLE

(From The Paramount Picture "THANKS FOR THE MEMORY")

Words by FRANK LOESSER
Music by HOAGY CARMICHAEL

Bb7 Bb7#5 Eb Gbdim7 Fm7 Fm7/Bb
Tick, tock! Cuck-oo! Here we are, out of cig-a-rettes,
Here we are, in the co-zy chair,
Eb Fm7 Fm7/Bb Bb7
hold-ing hands and yawn - ing, look how late it gets.
pick-ing on a wish - bone from the Frig-i-daire.
Eb C7 Fm7 Abm
Two sleep-y peo-ple by dawn's ear-ly light, and
Two sleep-y peo-ple with noth - ing to say, and
1
Eb F7 Fm7/Bb Bb7
too much in love to say "Good - night".

2
Eb
F7
Bb7
Eb
Eb7
3fr
too much in love to break a - way. Do you re -
Ab
Fm7
Bb7
Eb
Bb7
Eb
4fr
mem - ber the nights we used to lin - ger in the hall?
Cm
G7
Cm
Cm/Bb
Ab
Fm7
Bb7
Fa - ther did - n't like you at all. Do you re -
Eb
Bb7
Eb
Ddim7
C7
mem - ber the rea - son why we mar - ried in the fall? To

F7
Fm7
Bb7#5
rent this lit - tle nest, _ and get a bit of rest. Well,
Eb
Gbdim7
Fm7
Fm7/Bb
Bb7
Eb
3fr
here we are just a - bout the same, _ fog - gy lit-tle fel - la,
Fm7
Fm7/Bb
Bb7
Eb
C7
drows - y lit - tle dame. _ Two sleep - y peo - ple by
Fm7
Abm
4fr
Eb
F7
Bb7
Eb
Ab6
Eb
dawn's ear - ly light, and too much in love to say "Good-night".
3

WATCH WHAT HAPPENS

Music by MICHEL LEGRAND
Original French Text by JACQUES DEMY
English Lyrics by NORMAN GIMBEL

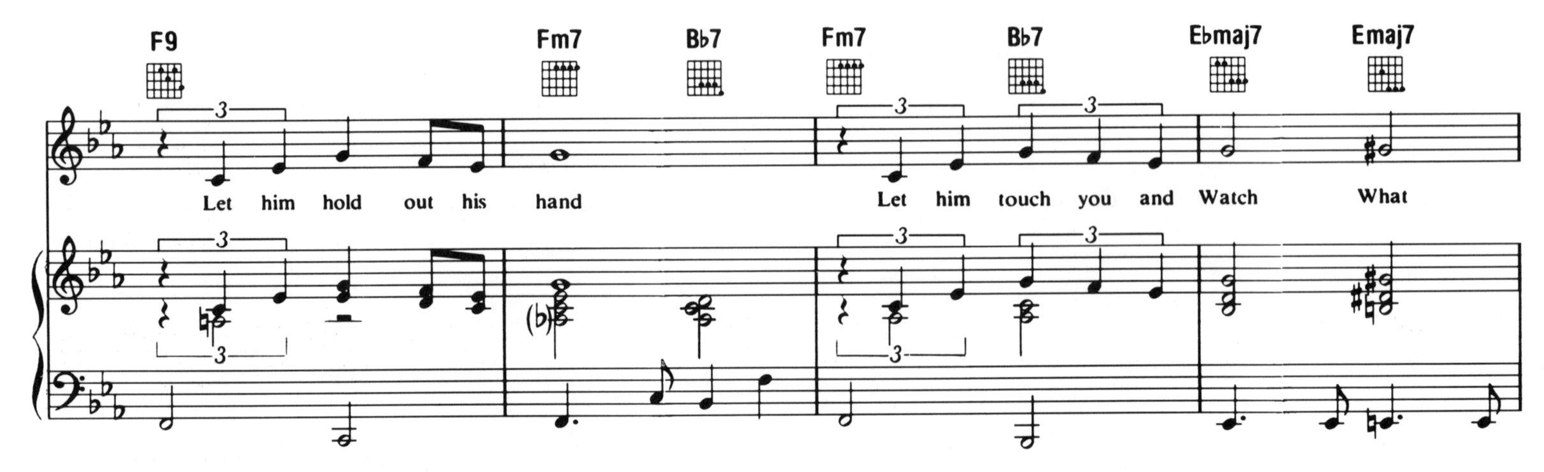

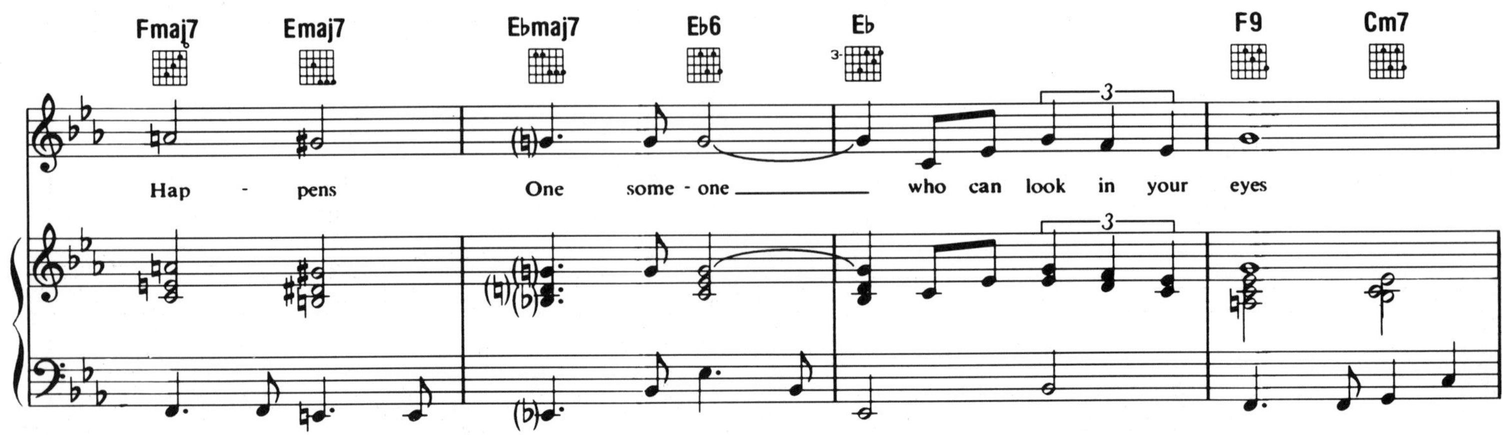

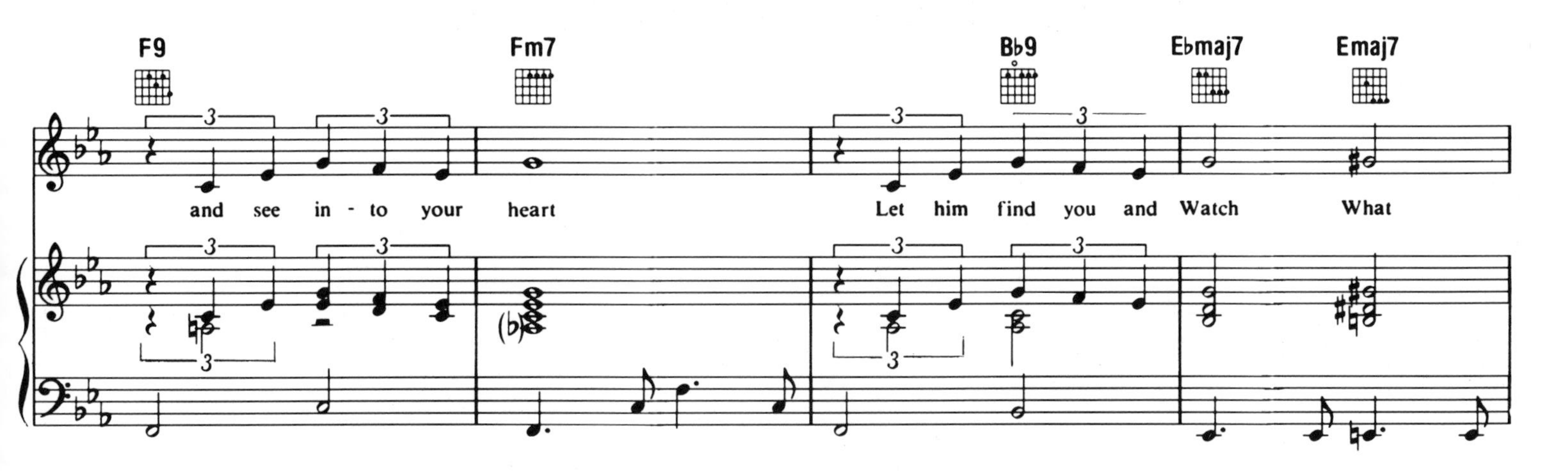
F9
Fm7
Bb9
Ebmaj7
Emaj7
and see in - to your heart
Let him find you and Watch What

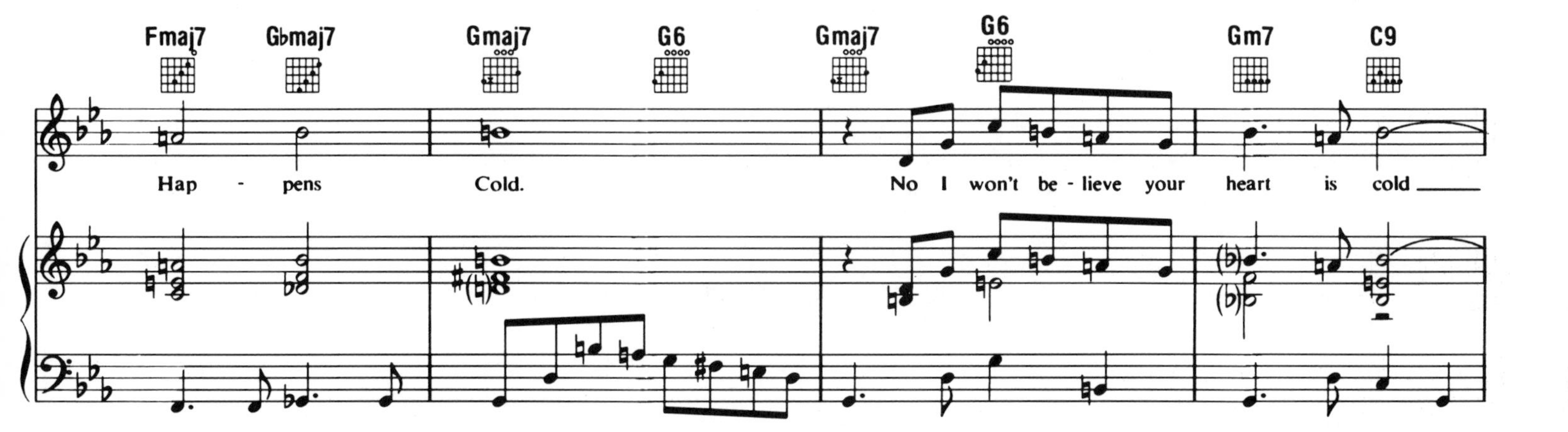
Fmaj7
Gbmaj7
Gmaj7
G6
Gmaj7
G6
Gm7
C9
Hap - pens Cold.
No I won't be - lieve your heart is cold

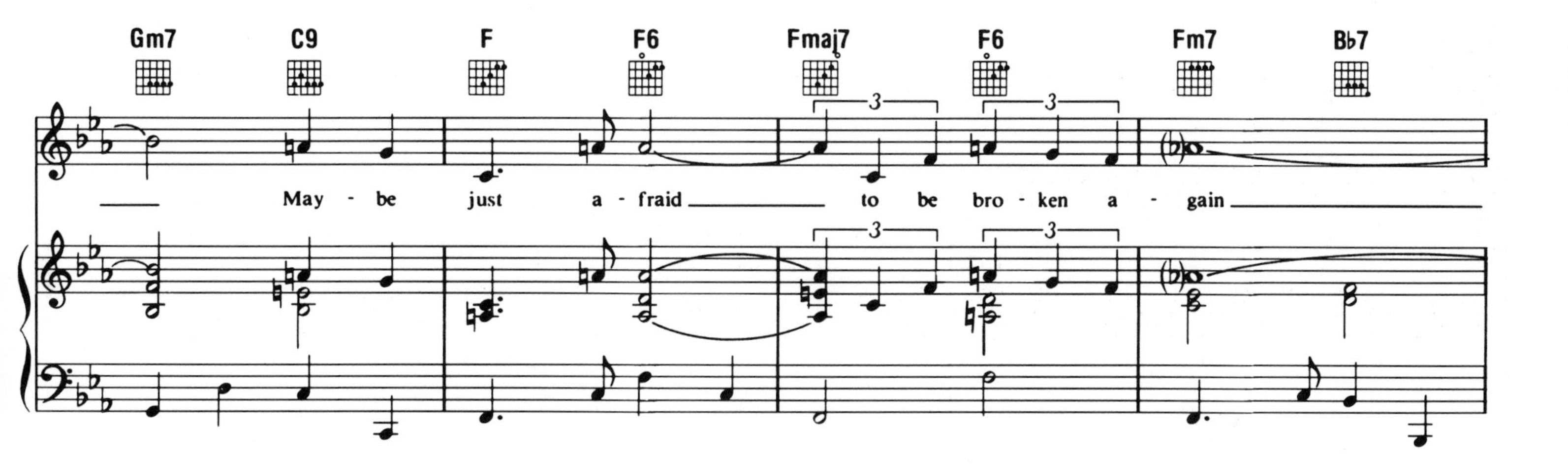
Gm7
C9
F
F6
Fmaj7
F6
Fm7
Bb7
May - be just a - fraid to be bro - ken a - gain

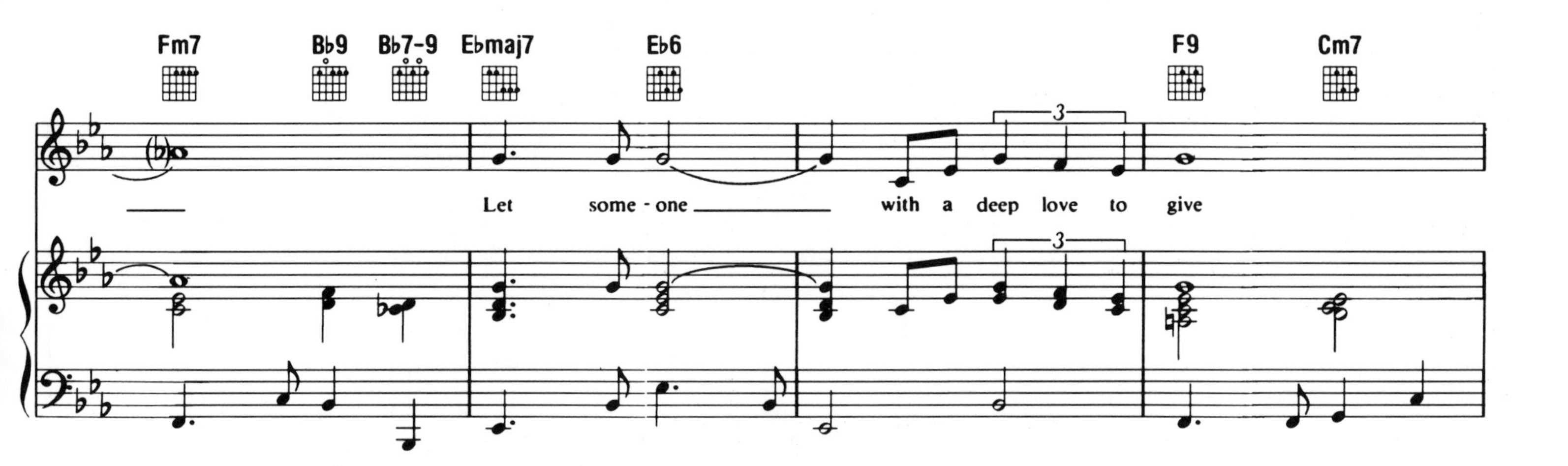
Fm7
Bb9
Bb7-9
Ebmaj7
Eb6
F9
Cm7
Let some - one with a deep love to give

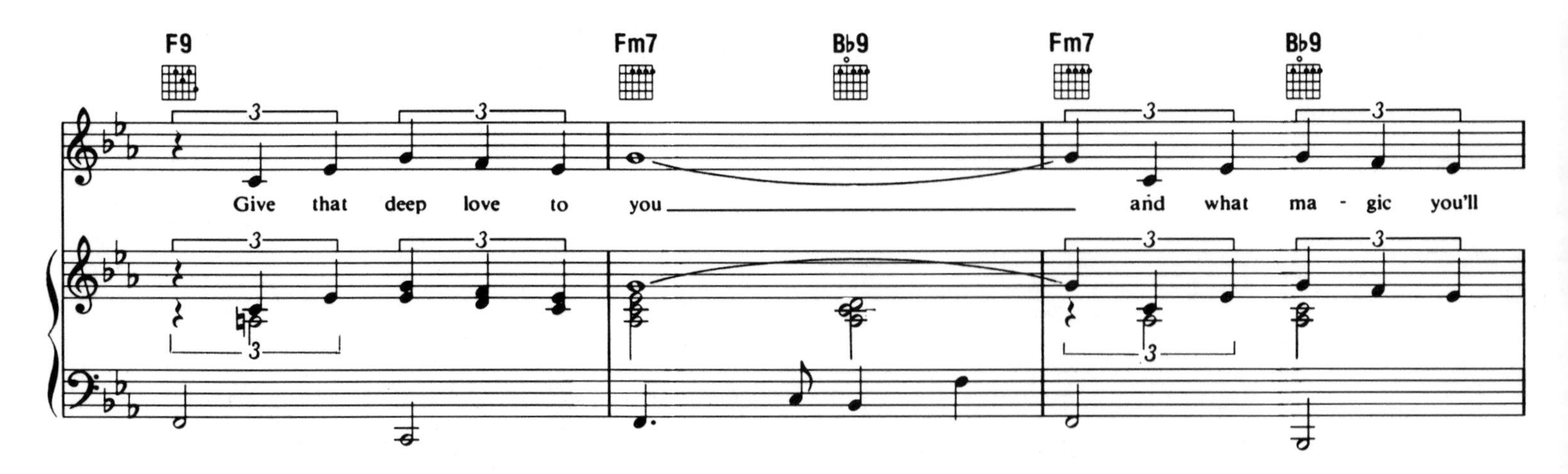
F9
Fm7
Bb9
Fm7
Bb9
Give that deep love to you and what ma - gic you'll

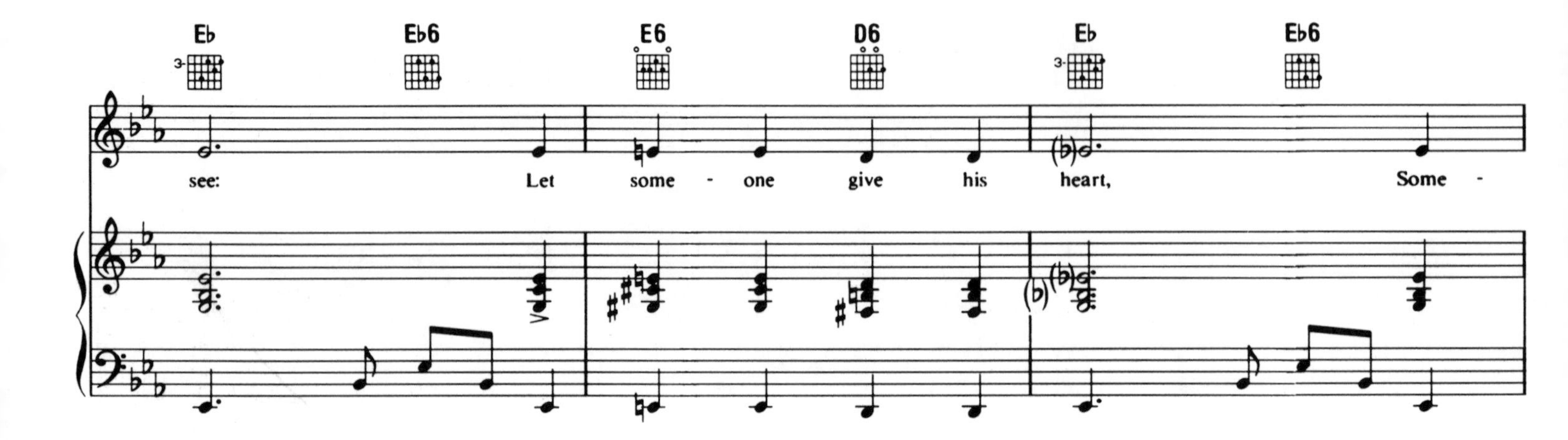
Eb
Eb6
E6
D6
Eb
Eb6
see: Let some - one give his heart, Some -

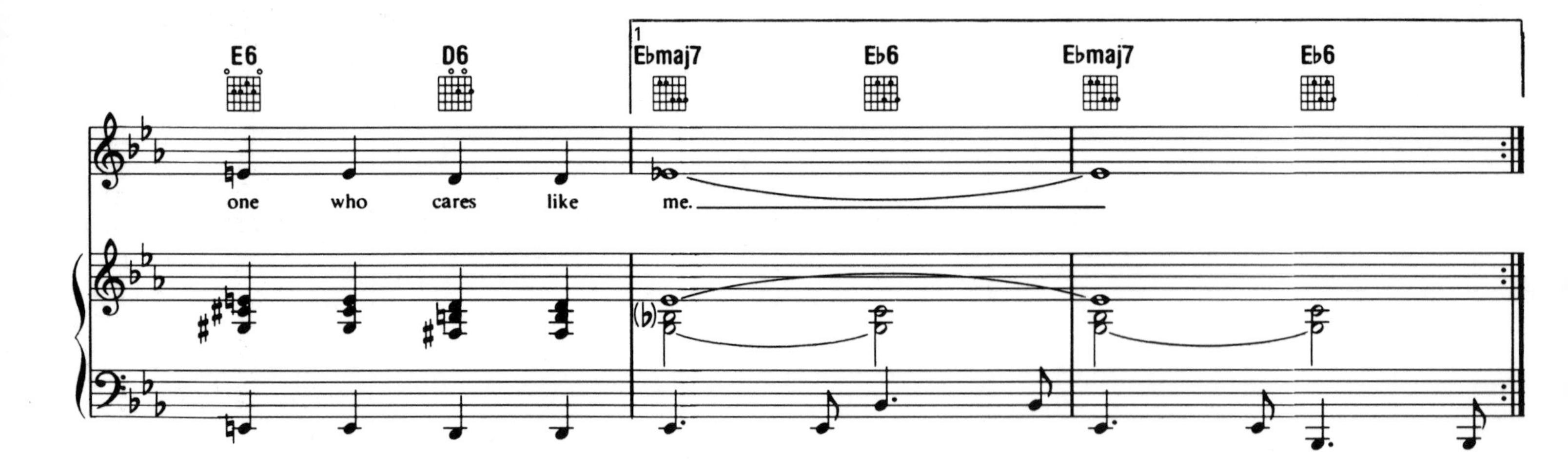
E6
D6
1
Ebmaj7
Eb6
Ebmaj7
Eb6
one who cares like me.

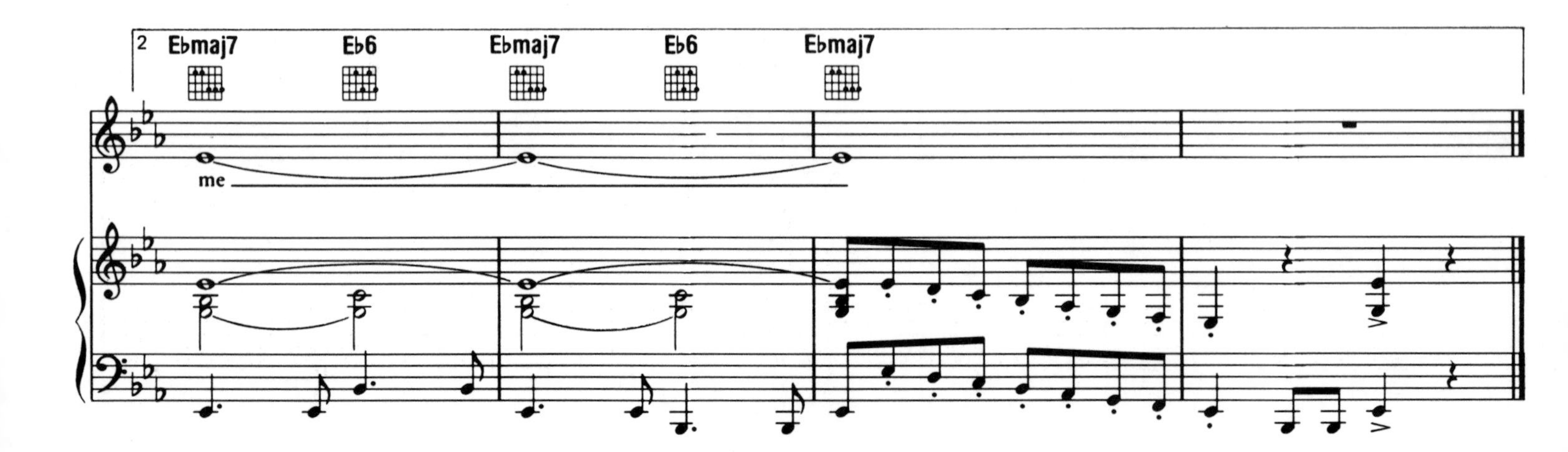
2
Ebmaj7
Eb6
Ebmaj7
Eb6
Ebmaj7
me

THE WAY WE WERE

(From The Motion Picture "THE WAY WE WERE")

Words by ALAN and MARILYN BERGMAN
Music by MARVIN HAMLISCH

Dmaj7
E7sus
E7
1
Amaj7
F♯m7
Bm7
D/E
of the way we were. Scat-tered
for the way we
2
Amaj7
A7
Dmaj7
C♯m7
Bm7
were.
Can it be that it was all so sim-ple then,
C♯m7
F♯7sus
F♯7
Bm7
Bm7/A
or has time re-writ-ten ev-'ry line?
If we had the chance to do it
E7sus
E7
Amaj7
D/E
E7
D.S. al Coda
all a-gain, tell me would we?
Could we?

CODA
Dmaj7
C♯7sus
C♯7
F♯m7
F♯m7/E
2fr
Dmaj7
we sim-ply choose to for - get.
So it's the
C♯m7
4fr
Dmaj7
C♯m7
4fr
laugh - ter we will re - mem - ber,
Dmaj7
C♯m7
4fr
F♯m7
Bm7
2fr
Bm7/E
when-ev - er we re - mem - ber the way we
Amaj7
Dmaj7
D/E
Amaj7
Dmaj7
Amaj7
were; the way we were.
rit.

WHAT NOW MY LOVE
(Original French Title: "ET MAINTENANT")

Original French Lyric by PIERRE DELANOE
Music by GILBERT BECAUD
English Adaptation by CARL SIGMAN

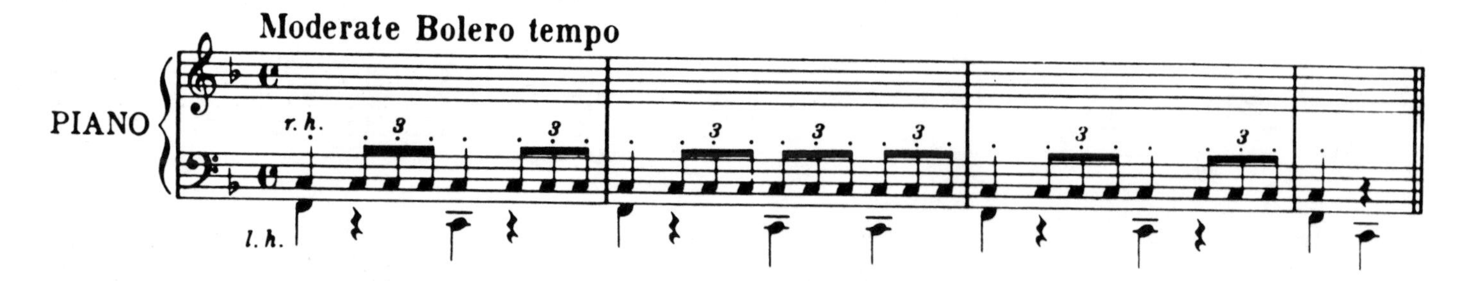

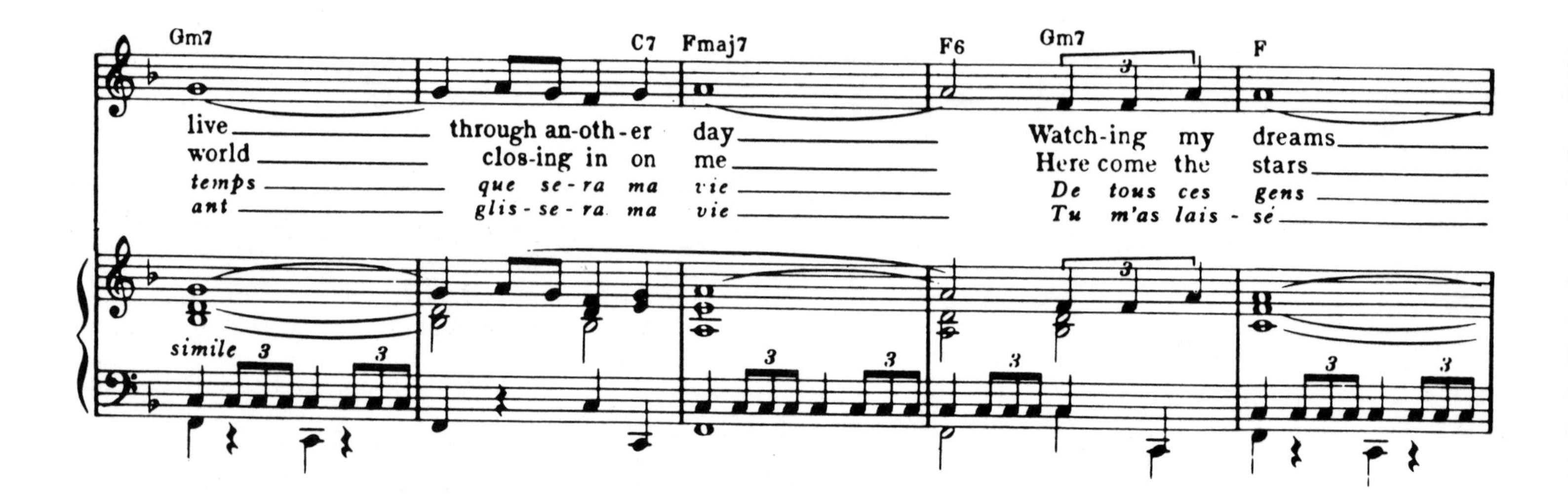

F Bb6 F6 Gm7 C7
Turn-ing to ash - es And my hopes in - to bits of
Tum-bling a - round me There's the sky where the sea should
qui m'in-dif-fe - rent Main-te-nant que tu es par -
la terre en-tiè - re Mais la terre sans toi c'est pe -

F Fmaj7 F7 Gm7 C7 Am7
clay Once I could see Once I could feel
be WHAT NOW MY LOVE Now that you're gone
tie Tou - tes ces nuits pour-quoi, pour qui
tit Vous mes a - mis soy - ez gen - tils

Dm7 Gm7 C7 Gm7 C7 F Fmaj7 F7
Now I am numb I've be-come un - real I walk the
I'd be a fool to go on and on No one would
Et ce ma - tin qui re - vient pour rien Mon coeur qui
Vous sa-vez bien que l'on n'y peut rien Mê - me Pa -

Bbm7 Eb7 Abmaj7 Dbmaj7 Db6 Bbm6
night With - out a goal Stripped of my heart,
care No one would cry If I should live
bat pour qui, pour - quoi Qui bat trop fort,
ris cre - ve d'en - nui Tou - tes ces rues

Bbm6
B°
Gm7
1. C7
Gm7
2 C7
Gm7
— my soul.
— or die.
— trop fort
— me tuent
WHAT NOW MY
ET MAIN-TE-
— WHAT NOW MY
— Je n'ai vrai-

F
Bb6
F6
Gm7
LOVE Now there is noth - ing On-ly my last
ment plus rien a fai - re Je n'ai vrai-ment
simile

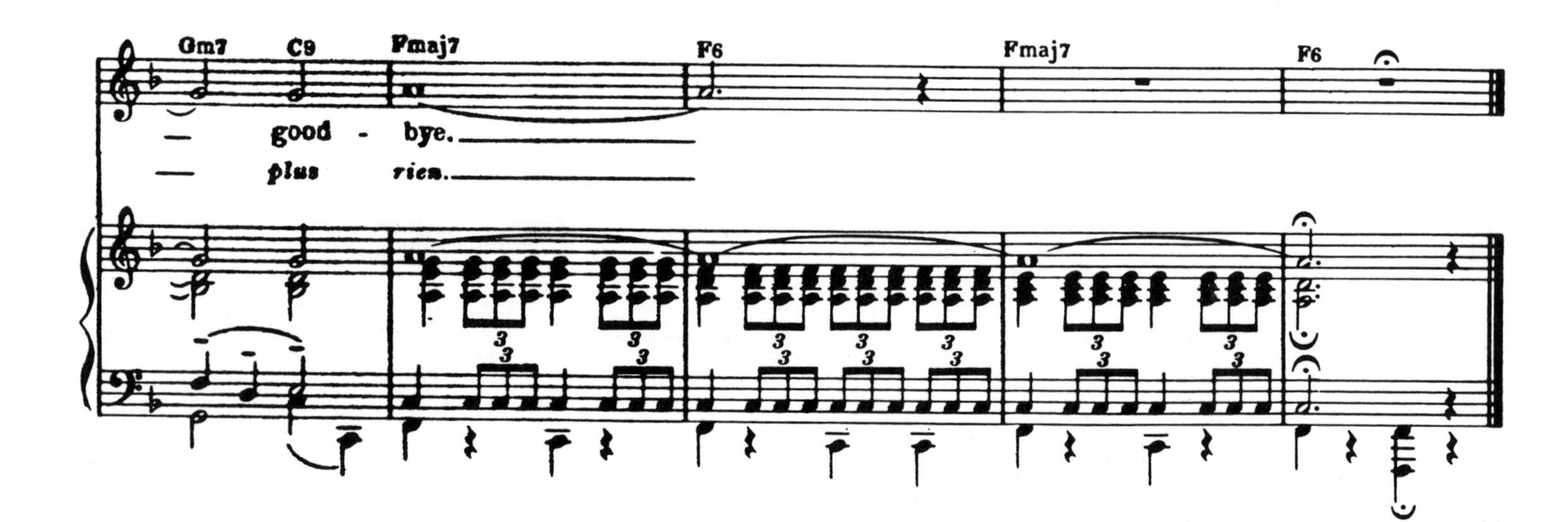
Gm7
C9
Fmaj7
F6
Fmaj7
F6
— good - bye.
— plus rien.

WHERE IS YOUR HEART
(THE SONG FROM MOULIN ROUGE)
(From "MOULIN ROUGE")

Words by WILLIAM ENGVICK
Music by GEORGE AURIC

Gm
Cm7
F7
Fm7/B♭
B♭7
this, I wor - ry and won - der. You're
Fm
B♭
Fm7
B♭6
B♭7
close to me here, but where is your
E♭
Fm7
B♭7
E♭maj7
E♭6
heart? It's a sad thing to re - al - ize that
Dm7♭5
G7
Cm
Am7♭5
D7♭9
you've a heart that nev - er melts. When we kiss, do you close your

Gm
Cm7
F7
B♭7
eyes, pre - tend - ing that I'm some - one else? You
E♭
Gm
Cm7
F7
Fm7/B♭
B♭7
must break the spell, this cloud that I'm un - der. So
Fm
Fm7/B♭
Edim7
Fm7
B♭6
B♭7
please won't you tell, dar - ling, where is your
1
E♭
B♭7
2
E♭
Fm7
E♭6
heart? When - heart?

WHO?

(From "SUNNY")

Words by OTTO HARBACH and OSCAR HAMMERSTEIN II
Music by JEROME KERN

Dm
E7
A7
Boy who'll know the an - swer when I ask.
Can be played with la - dies when they say:
D
Who stole my heart a - way?
A7
Who makes me dream all day? Dreams, I
know, can nev - er be true,
D
Seems as

A7
G
tho' I'll ev - er be blue. Who
mp

D
means my hap - pi - ness, Who would I an -

A7
- swer: yes, to?
Well you ought to guess
Darned if I can guess

D
1
2
who, no one but you.
who, no one but you.
p

WIVES AND LOVERS
(HEY, LITTLE GIRL)
(From The Paramount Picture "WIVES AND LOVERS")

Lyric by HAL DAVID
Music by BURT BACHARACH

Gm7
Gm9
C9
Cm7
you need-n't try an - y more.
For wives should
F7-9
Am7-5
D7
E♭ maj7
al - ways be lov - ers too.
Run to his
D7 (sus)
D7
D♭ maj7
arms the mo - ment he comes home to you.
I'm warn - ing
f
C7 (sus)
tacet
Fm7
Fm9
Fm7
you.
Day af - ter day there are
mp
mf

Fm9
Fm7
girls at the of - fice and men will al - ways be
Fm9
Gm7
Gm9
Gm7
men. Don't send him off with your
Gm9
Gm7
hair still in curl - ers, You may not see him a -
Gm9
C9
Cm7
F7-9
Am7-5
gain, for wives should al - ways be lov - ers

D7
E♭ maj7
D7 (sus)
too. Run to his arms the mo - ment he comes home to
D7
D♭ maj7
C7 (sus)
tacet
you. He's al - most here.
Fm7
Fm9
Fm7
Fm9
Hey, lit - tle girl, bet - ter wear some-thing pret - ty,
Fm7
B♭ 9
E♭ 6
E dim
some - thing you'd wear to go to the cit - y; And

Fm7
Fm9
Fm7
Fm9
dim all the lights, pour the wine, start the mu - sic,
Fm7
B♭9
E♭6
time to get read - y for love.
Oh,
Fm7
B♭9
Fm7
B♭9
time to get read - y, time to get read - y,
dim. poco a poco
Fm7
B♭9
E♭6
time to get read - y for love.
ppp
8va

YOU BROUGHT A NEW KIND OF LOVE TO ME

(From The Paramount Picture "THE BIG POND")

Words and Music by SAMMY FAIN,
IRVING KAHAL and PIERRE NORMAN

Bb 3b
7 5b Bb 3b
3
Ab
Fmin.
Ab 5♮
Ab
Fmin.
Ab 5♮
Ab
meet one sweet - er than you.
Ab 5♮
7 5b D 3♮
Would you turn a - way or could you real - ly learn to
Bb7
7 Bb 3b
poco rit.
Eb7
care If I'd ev - er dare to say, "I love you."
poco rit.
Ped.
*
REFRAIN
7 Bb 3b
a tempo
(not fast, with expression)
Eb7
Ab
Ab7
Bdim.
If the night - in - gales could sing like you They'd sing much sweet - er
p-mf a tempo

F7
Bb 3b 7
Eb 4 7
Eb 3 7
F 3b 7
than they do— For you've brought a new kind of love to me.
mf
Bb 3b 7
Eb7
Bb 3b 7
Eb7
Ab
Ab7
B dim.
If the sand-man brought me dreams of you— I'd want to sleep my
F7
Bb 3b 7
Eb 4 7
Eb 3 7
Ab
Bb 3b 5b 7
whole life thru,— For you've brought a new kind of love to me.
Ab
Bbmin.
Db7
Fmin.
C
Ab7
D 3♮ 5b 7
Bb7
Db7
C7
— I know that I'm the slave, you're the queen, But still you can un - der -
mf

Fmin. E♭ B♭5♯ Fdim. B♭7
stand That un-der-neath it all you're a maid And I am on - ly a
E♭7 D♭ E♭7 E♭7 A♭ A♭7 Bdim.
man. I would work and slave the whole day thru, If I could hur - ry
p
F7
home to you, For you've brought a new kind of love to
poco rit.
A♭ Adim. D♭ Adim. E♭7 A♭ A♭
me. If the me.
mf
a tempo

WRAP YOUR TROUBLES IN DREAMS
(AND DREAM YOUR TROUBLES AWAY)

Lyric by TED KOEHLER and BILLY MOLL
Music by HARRY BARRIS

Dm
G7♭9
4fr
C/E
E♭dim7
Dm7
E♭dim7
Love is hap - pi - ness! I've had hap - pi - ness
You can eas - i - ly Learn this mel - o - dy
C/E
Em7
A7♯5
but it end - ed one day.
What a won - der - ful song,
D9
4fr
Am7
D9
4fr
G
G7
Now I look at life a dif - f'rent way:
It will cheer you when the day is long:
Dm7/G
G9♯5
3fr
C6
G7
When skies are cloud - y and

C6
G7#5
C6
E7
Am7
gray, They're on - ly gray for a day, So
D9
4fr
Am7
Am/D
D7
wrap your trou - bles in dreams, And
Dm7/G
G7#5
C6
G9#5
3fr
C6
G7
dream your trou - bles a - way. Un - til that sun - shine peeps
C6
G7#5
C6
E7
thru, There's on - ly one thing to